# Sweet Cross

# SWEET CROSS

## A Marian Guide to Suffering

LAURA MARY PHELPS

Our Sunday Visitor
Huntington, Indiana

*Nihil Obstat*
Msgr. Michael Heintz, Ph.D.
*Censor Librorum*

*Imprimatur*
✠ Kevin C. Rhoades
Bishop of Fort Wayne-South Bend
July 21, 2021

The *Nihil Obstat* and *Imprimatur* are official declarations that a book is free from doctrinal or moral error. It is not implied that those who have granted the *Nihil Obstat* and *Imprimatur* agree with the contents, opinions, or statements expressed.

Except where noted, the Scripture citations used in this work are taken from the *Revised Standard Version of the Bible — Second Catholic Edition* (Ignatius Edition), copyright © 1965, 1966, 2006 National Council of the Churches of Christ in the United States of America. Used by permission. All rights reserved.

Our Sunday Visitor Publishing Division, Our Sunday Visitor, Inc., 200 Noll Plaza, Huntington, IN 46750; www.osv.com; 1-800-348-2440

ISBN: 978-1-68192-734-3 (Inventory No. T2604)
1. RELIGION—Christian Living—Spiritual Growth.
2. RELIGION—Christian Living—Inspirational.
3. RELIGION—Christianity—Catholic.

eISBN: 978-1-68192-735-0
LCCN: 2021940049

Cover and interior design: Lindsey Riesen
Cover art: Adobe Stock

PRINTED IN THE UNITED STATES OF AMERICA

*For my mother and father:*
*Thank you for your endless prayers and*
*giving me the sweetest gift a parent can give:*
*Mother Mary.*

# Contents

✝

# Introduction

Why is it that we can have total confidence and trust in God's plan for everyone else's life, but not for our own? It's easy for me to recognize God's hand in *your* life … in *your* misery … in *your* darkest season. But when suffering invites itself into my life? Not so easy. When God interrupts a perfectly good plan by sending a cross, I fail to see any reason for it. Instead of denying myself, picking up my cross, and following Jesus, I deny who God says he is, kick my cross, and eat my bodyweight in cheese.

Eating cheese is easier than suffering.

In the attempt to accept suffering, embrace my cross, and kick the cheese habit, I spent the summer of 2019 with the Blessed Mother. I managed to turn a thirty-three-day consecration into a four-month retreat because I'm *extra* like that. I knew that this consecration to Mary wasn't a magic trick that would make my suffering disappear; but to be honest, I kind of hoped that it would. In the deepest, most secret place of my brokenness, I prayed it would.

Spoiler alert: The suffering is still there. And thank God for that. But before you write me off as crazy, let me explain.

That summer with Mary was a game changer. For years, I'd been checking all the boxes that I thought needed to be checked to live a peaceful, saintly, trouble-free life (because saints don't suffer, right?). *Frequenting the sacraments?* Check! *Coordinating ministry?* Check! *Traveling to evangelize?* Check! *Praying the Rosary?* Check! But there was one box I refused to check, and it's really the most important box: *Willingly carrying my cross.* I just couldn't bring myself to do it. For starters, I didn't believe that living peacefully while suffering was possible. Kind of like keeping your eyes open while sneezing. But more importantly, I was afraid — something about that "willingly" part. If I were to accept my suffering willingly, Lord knows what other kinds of crazy things God would send my way. I didn't want to give him the impression that I was capable of suffering more than I was.

While I circled the cross, cheese knife in one hand, a hunk of cheddar in the other, Mother Mary flew to my side and remained there. During that four-month consecration, she slowly revealed the human Jesus to me. Not the plastic, cleaned up Jesus we keep in a drawer and take out when we need something, but the real, suffering Jesus, who by his death on the cross has already given us all that we need. In meeting Christ face to face this way, I finally met myself and discovered the truth of the cross and the sweetness of suffering.

Mother Teresa wore a cross pendant that illustrates this very real sweetness of the cross. It's called the Unity Cross, and it depicts Jesus on a low cross, enabling Mary to be pressed against him as she collects his blood in a chalice. Mother Teresa said this cross best expressed what she and her community wanted to do: "Like Mary to stand by the Cross of the Dying Christ and to meet him there."

For years, I prayed to meet Jesus. I wanted to meet healing Jesus. Miracle-working Jesus. I wanted to encounter the Jesus who turns water into wine and makes me breakfast on the beach. Party

Jesus. I have no problem loving this Jesus. But I hesitated to get close to suffering Jesus. Sweating-blood Jesus. Scourged Jesus. Disfigured Jesus. Humiliated Jesus. Crucified Jesus. Dying Jesus.

The reality is that, as Catholics, we don't proclaim a cut-and-paste faith. If we want to follow Jesus, we must follow all of him. We don't get to choose the parts of him we like and cut and throw away the rest. The Jesus who invites us to recline with him at table is the same Jesus who invites us to embrace and stand with his mother at the foot of the cross. Oh, how we love to kneel and adore sweet baby Jesus in the wood of the manger! But do we love to follow that same baby to the wood of the cross?

It wasn't until I placed myself next to Mary and resolved to walk it out with her that my heart and mind were opened to a whole new perspective. To comprehend the love God has for me, I needed to lean into my Mother. To carry my cross without fear or complaint, I needed to imitate Mary. I needed to behold her. Why? Because Jesus commanded so while hanging on the cross: "Behold, your mother" (Jn 19:27). And this isn't just true for me; it's true for all of us. We need our heavenly mother because there's no greater human example of how and why we suffer.

But what does it look like to walk this road with Mary? We must first behold her and let her show us who God is; and then we need to imitate her. That's why we will embark in this book on a journey of learning how to embrace our cross by imitating Mary's ten principal virtues, as described by St. Louis de Montfort in his beautiful book, *True Devotion to Mary*. De Montfort writes, "Our Mother is also a perfect mold wherein we are to be molded in order to make her intentions and dispositions ours." What better to fill this mold than Mary's virtues, "her sentiments, her actions, her participation in the mysteries of Christ and her union with Him?"

De Montfort says that, in addition to acts of love and pious affection for the Blessed Virgin, we must imitate Our Lady's virtues if we are to grow in faith. I'll give a fair warning: None of this is easy. However, nothing good for us ever is. So don't let that disturb you. We'll take it slowly, one virtue at a time.

It might be helpful to start with a quick refresher on virtue. What is virtue? According to the *Catechism of the Catholic Church*, a virtue is "an habitual and firm disposition to do the good. It allows the person not only to perform good acts, but to give the best of himself. The virtuous person tends toward the good with all his sensory and spiritual powers; he pursues the good and chooses it in concrete actions. The goal of a virtuous life is to become like God" (1803).

Because she is perfect, Mary perfectly exemplifies all the virtues. St. Louis de Montfort describes ten of these virtues as the specific characteristics of Our Lady that we should aim to emulate. These ten principal virtues of Mary are:

- Lively faith
- Ardent charity
- Divine wisdom
- Heroic patience
- Profound humility
- Angelic sweetness
- Surpassing purity
- Blind obedience
- Universal mortification
- Constant mental prayer

In this book, we'll go into each of these ten virtues in depth. I've also added three more — unshakable confidence, unwavering trust, and firm peace — because these are virtues I've needed in learning to embrace my cross, and I don't think I'm alone in that. Mary exemplifies these virtues perfectly. We'll discuss these extras in chapters 1, 4, and 7.

Living out these virtues enabled Mary to endure her cross. If we ask her, Mary will pray for us to receive the grace of obtaining and putting these same virtues into practice in our lives, too. Why does this matter? Because suffering is real, my friend, and I've got news for you: It's here to stay. Not continuously, of course. Like the flowers and trees, it has its seasons. Yet we cannot avoid it, and more than that, it's a necessary part of the Christian life that comes with benefits and merits and gets us to heaven.

Suffering can go one of two ways: It can excite you and motivate you to move forward in faith, or it can depress you and motivate you to pull the covers up over your head and wish to die. I tried this second method, and I can share with confidence that it doesn't work. Not only did I not die, but when I got out of bed, I discovered the dishes had not been done and the dog had peed on the couch, and none of that was getting me to heaven.

As Christians, we want heaven. We want to be with Jesus for eternity. Mary's virtues offer us the support we need beneath our crosses, and the strength we need to follow Jesus all the way to heaven. Taking Mary's virtues on as our own offers us a whole new way of looking at the cross, helping us to embrace our suffering.

I know. You don't want to embrace the suffering. You want to set it on fire. Maybe you don't believe that suffering is something we should have to endure, or that it serves any good purpose. Maybe you're frustrated because suffering is just plain uncomfortable, and you don't even know how to respond to it. Maybe, like me, you don't want other people to know that you're suffering. For a long while, I believed that talking about my suffering meant admitting my weakness. And I had way too much pride to admit that. Yet what I discovered was that not accepting my suffering made the suffering worse. Hiding my suffering in an attempt to look pulled together weakened me. Trust me: We do no one any favors by pretending our lives are untouched by suffering.

In his book *The Imitation of Christ*, Thomas à Kempis writes, "No remedy or comfort can free you from this affliction or make it easier for you to bear; you simply have to bear your cross as long as God wills it." And well, let's be honest, that sounds terrible. You picked up this book because you were hoping it was going to give you the formula to rid your life of suffering, or at the very least, offer a few techniques that teach you how to breathe your suffering away. If the quick fix is what you're after, I'm sorry to say that you won't find it hidden in these pages. There are some sufferings that a comfort dog or yoga class just won't reach.

But if you're looking to meet Jesus amid his suffering so that you can better understand your own; if running from the truth of your trial has left you exhausted, and you're ready to find a new way to live; if you're so beaten down by the blows of life that your faith is hanging on by a thread, then I urge you to stay with me. Go ahead and keep eating the cheese and crack open that third beer, but please stay. Because if this is where you are, I know that place well. I've lived there, only it wasn't really living.

And I promise you this: While I can't remove the cross for you, I can help you carry it. You don't have to be afraid, because we don't approach the cross alone. We've got our mother Mary to guide us and protect us every step of the way; and who doesn't need their mother? By diving deeply into one of Mary's virtues in each chapter in this book, we'll learn to imitate her in gladly embracing hardship, recognizing that things that appear to be obstacles to the good life are really an invitation to enter into it.

I debated writing this book for years. Suffering is personal. It's hard. And exposing it can feel as enjoyable as a colonoscopy. But it's time for us to get uncomfortable. We can't outrun our cross, so we might as well start carrying it. So what do you say we do this together, arm in arm with Mama Mary? Let's approach our suffering in a whole new way, falling so deeply in love with all of Jesus that there's no place we would rather be than pressed up against him at the foot of the cross.

— 1 —

# Embracing Your Cross with Unshakable Confidence

✝

I've always been afraid. Terrified, actually. Of what, you ask? Good grief, so many things, big and little. You name it, and I'm probably afraid of it.

I'm afraid of the dark, noises in the night, and going blind.

I'm afraid of the ocean and being eaten by a shark.

I'm afraid of driving at night, driving in the rain, and driving in the snow.

I'm afraid of driving off a bridge and getting trapped in my car underwater (or of escaping through the car window and being eaten by a shark).

I'm afraid of the phone ringing. Calls from the school. Calls from the police. Calls from my children. Calls, period.

And I'm afraid of receiving texts. Texts in the middle of the night. Texts in the morning. Texts in the afternoon. Group texts. (Okay, so technically, I am not afraid of group texts. I just find them incredibly annoying. I'm convinced that hell is just one never-ending group text that you can't ever leave or put on "do not disturb." And everybody "likes" everything. For eternity.)

I'm afraid of loud noises. Sudden movements. Alarms. Sirens. Earthquakes.

And when my husband climbs a shaky ladder. Or a sturdy ladder. Can he please just not go on ladders?

I'm afraid of having no money.

I'm afraid of losing my husband (because he fell off a ladder) and being left with the kids, mortgage, car payment, grilling, lawn mowing, and Saturday dump runs.

I'm afraid of looking stupid. Of people noticing I have no idea what I'm doing. Of being criticized. Of people "figuring me out." Of being misunderstood. Of being forgotten.

I'm afraid of losing my children, physically and spiritually. I'm afraid of waking up to find only two cars in the driveway, instead of three. I'm afraid of being kidnapped and locked in a trunk. I'm afraid of math, spreadsheets, and being called on when I don't know the answer.

I'm afraid of hell. And all-you-can-eat salad bars. Maybe hell is actually an all-you-can-eat salad bar … while receiving a never-ending group text.

This litany of fears isn't a joke. Not too long ago, I lived in Code Red pretty much all the time. Never mind that we're commanded over 300 times in Scripture to "be not afraid." Never mind that some of the things I fear are highly unlikely to happen to me. The truth is that the "unlikely to happen" has already happened. That thing that happens to "other people" happened to my family. And so, I began to fear that everything, no matter how crazy, is likely to happen. And that scared me.

It was a picture-perfect Friday morning in December. There was a lot of excitement brewing in our house. Christmas was just two weeks away. My son Luke's first-grade class would be making their famous gingerbread houses on this day. I was actually supposed to volunteer with his class that morning, but my husband and I had a special trip planned, so I'd gotten someone else to substitute for me. After the last school bus stop run of the morning, Nick and I were packing our bags and heading out for a night in New York City — the city where we met, fell in love, got married, and had our first baby. The hotel was booked, the fridge was stocked, and the babysitting covered. Everything was perfectly planned and in place.

I forgot to add one other important fear of mine to the list earlier: the fear that my husband and I go out of town without our children, get into a car accident, and die with no will, leaving them orphans. And so, as the school bus came rolling down the hill, I turned to my little ones, zipped up their coats, and made the Sign of the Cross on their foreheads, blessing them while praying, "I pray that God sends all of his angels to protect you today." In truth, I wasn't afraid for them, but for me. What if something happened to me? Who would clip their fingernails? Does my husband even know that they have fingernails? What if something happened to both of us?

Back at the house, I remember two things: eyeliner and the phone call. Envisioning a day of shopping and dining without kids, I felt the urge to apply heavy black eyeliner. I know. I'm wild like that. What's truly wild is that I remember that moment — what I was wearing, how I was standing, leaning into the mirror, with a thick black eye pencil in my hands. I even remember thinking that I should hurry it up so we could get on the road, ignoring the urgency, and staying in front of the mirror. Then the phone call came. Just as we were about ready to head out the door, a call from Newtown Public Schools appeared on my phone. I shot my husband a look, because a call from the school is never good. Either someone did something stupid on the bus, or someone was sick. My thirteen-year-old happened to be home sick from school that morning, so one of the little ones could now be sick as well. I could leave the teenager home alone until my parents arrived, but not Luke or Annie. While I didn't know why the phone was ringing, I feared I already knew enough: Our plans were about to get complicated.

But it wasn't the nurse. In fact, it wasn't even a person. It was a voice recorded message, and I struggled to make sense of it. Something about a suspected shooting in one of our schools … or was it in the neighborhood of one of the schools? And something about all the children being put in lock down and to please stay tuned for further details. Or something like that. I know: You'd think that I'd remember that message word for word. But I don't. In fact, that call was the beginning of many details I cannot recall.

If you've ever experienced trauma, you understand that memory loss is a natural survival skill and defense mechanism we develop to protect ourselves from psychological damage. To this day, my husband will tell you details of that day that I would swear never happened, and vice versa. The only occurrence of that day that I'm 100 percent certain of is this: At the exact moment I was supposed to be with my children at their school, a gunman forced his way in and murdered twenty first graders and six adult educators. Instead of being with my son in his classroom at the most terrifying moment of his life, I was at home, oblivious, carefully applying eyeliner.

We were in the dark, unaware of the magnitude of that morning's tragic event for quite some time. While the world was brought to its knees, planted in front of screens, we were in the center of the arena, scrambling to make sense of the situation, uncertain of what we were supposed to do next. As bits and pieces started to come into play, my husband wanted to head straight for the elementary school, which was just down the road from us. But that sounded risky to me. I was too afraid of getting in the way. What if there *was* a shooter? What if there were *many* shooters? What if they were running through Sandy Hook village? Plus, I'm a rule follower. If the kids were in lock down, that meant we were being asked to stay put. I suggested we go to the church and pray, and so we got in the car, bringing our oldest, Jack, along for the ride. With a possible shooter on the loose, I was afraid to leave him at home alone. The lack of control I had over the situation was shredding my insides.

As we drove to St. Rose of Lima Church, calls and texts began to blow up my phone; friends in town were reporting the "news" they heard on Facebook: "Two men with guns are at Sandy Hook School!" The minute-by-minute report was not helpful, nor was it true. Friends two thousand miles away were reaching out, asking if my kids were OK, appearing to have far more information than we did. Streets were blocked off by police, forcing us to take the back roads, adding minutes that felt like hours to our drive. I could see a small group of moms huddled by their cars as we pulled into the church parking lot. I got out of the car and walked quickly to the doors, devastated to discover that children were inside, and the church, too, was on lock down. I couldn't get to the school. I couldn't get into church. I couldn't get to my children. So I ran to where I knew I'd be let in.

I ran to my Mother Mary.

There's a statue of Our Lady outside of our church. Set against a backdrop of pine trees that block the view of a gas station, she stands there peacefully, with hands folded in prayer while her heel crushes the head of the serpent like a total badass. She has no eyeballs, and I'm not going to lie — that kind of freaks me out. But she is beautiful, nonetheless. If anyone can pull off no eyes, it's Mary. I got down on my knees on the cement ground and folded my hands in prayer. I prayed, *Please, Mary, keep my children safe.* Having no idea what to do or where to go, I probably could've stayed there on my knees for hours. It's where I felt safe. But my husband's impulse was to search and rescue. So despite our instructions to stay still, we headed toward Sandy Hook School, on a mission to find our children and bring them home.

In the non-stop flurry of ever-changing news, we'd been told that one person had been shot inside the school. But as we sped toward Sandy Hook School, ambulance after ambulance raced by. If only one person had been shot, why so many ambulances? I looked to my husband for help. He'd been searching the internet, learning more information than I had, but he was keeping it to himself to protect me. "This isn't for one person," I said. And like a cinematic flashback, every event of the day until that hideous moment played back before my eyes: zipping up coats, blessing their foreheads, praying for God's protection. I asked on repeat, "Do you think they're dead? Do you think they're dead?" I was certain that my bus stop prayer had been a final goodbye. I feared that my two littlest ones were gone.

With no way to get close to the school, my husband, now on the verge of vomiting, finally just parked the car on the street, got out, and ran to find his children. I waited it out for a bit with Jack. He was afraid and started to ask me, "Mom, are they alive?" and I honestly didn't know how to answer him. Before long I couldn't take it any longer, and so I told Jack to get out with me and run. As we made our way over to the school, my phone rang. It was Nick. The children were all at the firehouse just at the end of the road. "I found Luke ... Luke is here with his class," he said, catching his breath. "But I can't find Annie. I don't see her." Jack and I made it to the firehouse, where we searched faces and pushed through crowds until at last my eyes landed on her; she was standing there in the middle of the mess with her class, no winter coat on, talking to a friend. I ran to her, got down low, cupped her face in my hands, and started to cry. She looked at me and smiled, the kind of smile she gives when something is wrong but she doesn't want to acknowledge it. She asked, "Why are you crying, Mom?" in a silly voice, one that let me know she was pretending to be OK.

A few lines of children away, Luke was talking to a classmate and eating animal crackers out of a clear dixie cup. His teacher stood at the head of the line, holding a piece of paper that read GRADE 1. She looked like a ghost. All the color had drained from her face, and she barely moved or spoke, but she let me know with her eyes that something unimaginable had just occurred inside that school. And sweet Jack, my teenage boy who had to accompany his parents on the worst journey of their lives, stood off alone in that firehouse and broke down in tears. It was the first and last time I would see him cry over that terrible, unforgettable day.

One of Saint Rose's newest and youngest priests worked his way through the crowd. As we made eye contact, he asked me if I'd found my children. I was running on such adrenaline that I didn't piece together why a priest was necessary. I'd not yet made the connection that not every mother at the firehouse was going to leave with her child — that some parents' arms were going home empty that day. No one really knew what was happening, not even our two kids who'd been there for it. Annie told us she heard that a bear was set loose in the school. "They said, 'Release the bear!'" she told us with wide eyes, while Luke carried on as if nothing had happened and just wanted to know if we could go back to his classroom to get his coat and backpack. "We can go back and get your stuff later," I promised, as we made our way back to the car. But we never went back to that school ever again.

The months to follow were some of the darkest, most frightening, and most chaotic I've ever had to endure. Conspiracy theorists (or "truthers") added to our trauma with their false and outrageous claim that the Sandy Hook shooting was a hoax, and that both my husband and I were actors in a make-believe tragedy. They slandered our names, threatened our lives, and terrorized my family. Confusion and panic, on top of the shock and grief, became too much to bear. Questions I initially refrained from asking eventually grew too loud to ignore. Questions like, Why would you allow this, Lord? Why wouldn't you stop this?

The enemy kept my focus locked on the crisis, not on Christ. By dwelling on my circumstance, always thinking of what might happen next, I lost sight of the grace that Jesus was offering — the grace for the day. Instead of staying focused on what I knew about God, I chose to focus on what I didn't know about the future. I dwelt on the "why?" and "what if?," refusing God's grace. In reaching for fear, I let go of faith because I lacked what was needed to embrace this cross: unshakable confidence in God.

## Mary's Unshakable Confidence

The angel Gabriel told the Virgin Mary that she had been chosen by God to be the mother of the Messiah. This is my favorite Bible story (and Rosary mystery), because I feel like I can sit in that moment with Mary and say, "Oh, girl. I feel ya." Not because I've ever seen an angel (I haven't). And not because I've ever been asked to carry the Son of God (although my two boys are pretty spectacular). But because I've experienced that moment of God breaking through my well laid out plans and inviting me into his plan: a plan that comes with no guarantee, and requires total surrender. Yet in Mary's case, it's not so much that things fell through as *God broke through*. This is how her Annunciation applies to our lives as well. Because when plans and expectations fall through, that's precisely the moment when God breaks through.

The question is: How are we to respond? Mary could have said, "No." Or, at the very least, "I'm not so sure, can I get back to you on this?" Or, "Wait, what? Right now? I'm sorry, but I'm crazy busy this week …" Because this encounter of the angel with Mary was a scary big deal. If it weren't, why would Mary have been "greatly troubled"? Why would Gabriel tell her, "Do not be afraid"? This is important: Choosing not to be afraid doesn't suggest that we aren't scared. So how did Mary do it? Where did her courage come from? How did she keep from allowing her emotions to steer the ship? Confronted by God and *his* plan for her life, Mary did three things before giving her answer, and these three things demonstrated her unshakable confidence.

First, Mary listened to the voice of God.

How did Mary recognize his voice? She had spent time in his Word. We know this from her Magnificat, where she alludes to a variety of Old Testament texts: She references Deuteronomy, which recounts how the Lord's arm was powerful to save; she draws on the psalms that rejoice in the goodness and loving-kindness of the Lord, and point out his faithfulness to all generations. Mary could recognize God's voice because she was well versed in Scripture.

It's God's voice alone that inspires courage. We can hustle, strive, white knuckle, even numb our way through life, but unless we listen to the voice of the One who holds all things together, we'll never tap into the grace that only he can bestow — the grace that we need to respond to our call fearlessly. It's not enough to know about God; we must enter into a relationship with him. We do this by studying Scripture.

Second, Mary asked good questions.

When Mary asked, "How can this be?" she wasn't doubting God's plan, but she did want to understand what was needed from her to make it happen. Mary had confidence in God's plan for her. Unlike Eve, who listened to the voice of the serpent in the garden, leading her to doubt God's goodness and choose sin over paradise, Mary neither hesitated nor wavered. She listened, asked questions, and connected what she knew from Scripture to what God was asking of her. Make no mistake: Mary's questions are questions of faith.

Fr. Peter Cameron illustrates the beauty of the Annunciation in his book *Mysteries of the Virgin Mary: Living Our Lady's Graces*:

Before all else, in the angel's astounding proposal Mary perceives not a problem she needs to solve but the Mystery who chooses her. This is why the method of the Annunciation remains the norm for the Christian faith. For faith is not something that I think up; it is not the fruit of analysis. Neither does faith equal "keeping rules": It is not the result of my initiative to get close to God; it is not the outcome of my "ethical excellence." Faith is a response to something that happens outside of me. Faith entails acknowledging an exceptional presence that chooses to come to me — a presence that radically changes my life, infusing it with an intensity and fullness I cannot bring about on my own.

Third, Mary accepted the invitation.

I love John Bartuneck's explanation of Mary's response in his book *The Better Part*: "She accepted the angel's message and all its implications for her own life — a radical, unforeseen change in her plans. She was able to do so because she had long ago assimilated a doctrine we too often ignore, one that Gabriel reminded her of: 'Nothing is impossible for God.'" Believing this, knowing and trusting in God's Word, was and is everything. Love, not fear, was the driving force behind her *fiat*. Believing that God was who he said he was, and that any burden he permits is part of a bigger plan — bigger than we could ever dream up or imagine — Mary could echo the Prophet Isaiah in saying, "Behold, God is my salvation; / I will trust, and will not be afraid" (Is 12:2).

In the aftermath of the Sandy Hook School shooting, I was confident of only one thing: I was afraid. It's not that I wanted to lose confidence in God and remain afraid, but that I'd already developed that habit. I was used to operating out of a spirit of fear. As the days unfolded, and fake news about my husband and me started to spread, my habit of "run and hide" kicked into full gear. I pulled the plug on my writing and shut down all social media accounts. Trolls were surrounding me, digging and searching up anything they could get their hands on. It was unbelievable to me that such people existed. I pulled all the curtains shut and periodically peeked out the windows, looking for suspicious people and unfamiliar cars. If my husband traveled, I slept with every light on. This was also the beginning of my never answering the phone ever again. To this day, I get a pit in my stomach when it rings. If you were planning on calling me, please don't. And don't surprise me by coming over, either, because guess what? I'm afraid of that too. Basically, if you want to reach me, your safest bet is via pigeon carrier. I've yet to have a negative experience with a pigeon. But never say never, right?

Still, we have to remember something: Feeling afraid isn't a sin. Feeling scared doesn't make us bad Christians. We're not our feelings. In fact, God tells us not to be afraid because he knows that we will be! This is why, in times of fear, I'm especially drawn to Jesus' command, "Take heart, it is I; have no fear" (Mk 6:50). While we feel fear, courage is ours for the taking. Courage is what allows us to act even in the face of our uncertainty. And what we learn from the Annunciation is that we can respond confidently and without fear in any situation, because we have a God who calls us by name (see Is 43:1), just as the angel greeted Our Lady: "Hail, Mary!"

The same God that broke into Mary's life thousands of years ago breaks into our lives today. He calls us by name and offers us courage, assuring us that it is he, God our Savior, and we do not need to be afraid.

We learn Mary's unshakable confidence as we adjust our view of God. What's your view of God? Does your confidence lie in him and what he can do, or have you taken that responsibility for yourself? True confidence has nothing to do with developing more confidence in ourselves, but actually less. We don't achieve unshakable confidence because of something we've done, but because of who God is. We can only live confidently and unafraid when we stop believing that we are in control. We must put God in his rightful place, step the heck out of his way, and trust that he knows what he's doing. It means we walk by faith, not looking to what we see but rather to what God is doing — even if we're convinced he's doing nothing at all. And we never ask, "Why?" but we do ask, "How?"

Mary knew that our security should never lie in ourselves, but only in the Lord (see Ps 4:8). No matter how impossible the request, she believed in the One asking. Mary also knew the importance of keeping her eyes on today, living for the present moment, and resisting the temptation to look at tomorrow. Fear keeps us in pursuit of false safety. We think that if only we could control everything, we'd have no anxiety and rest in true inner peace. Yet this couldn't be any farther from the truth. The unbroken peace and undisturbed rest we seek aren't to be found here on earth, but in heaven. Every time we desire to know the future more than we trust God, we forget about why we run this race in the first place.

Every time we allow fear to convince us that the suffering God permits us is unreasonable, impossible, and unfair, we choose the temporary over the everlasting. Heaven is our goal, and confidence in our Maker is what leads us to the reward. Mary's eagerness for heaven greatly outweighed her desire for earthly comfort and understanding.

May we pray for that same eagerness and confidence.

## — 2 —

# Embracing Your Cross with Lively Faith

✝

L et's talk turkey. How many times have you asked God, "Why?"
Why me?

Why now?

Why this?

Why that?

Why my kids?

Why my marriage?

Why, why, why???

"Why" is my go-to response to suffering. That and "Are you kidding me?" The problem with asking God "why" is that we rarely get an answer. And let's be honest: If he did give an answer, would we really be OK with it?

When my husband implied that we might need to confront our high school-aged son about experimenting with drugs, I was honestly blindsided. Call me naive, but I had no idea. When my husband's suspicion became a hard reality and addiction worked its way into our story, my entire world fell apart. Where my husband took the "he'll grow out of this phase" approach, I fell into a world of worst-case scenarios and desperately needed to understand why. *Why my son? Why us, his parents? Why?* I tortured myself with why. I knew in my head that God's ways were not my ways, nor his understanding anywhere near close to my understanding, but my heart had yet to buy into this verse as being anything other than annoying. Like a dog chasing its tail, I ran in circles around what I needed to accept out of pure faith.

The reality? Addiction was a thread that found its way into my family's tapestry, and due to my lack of acceptance, that thread would become a tight noose around my neck. The more I demanded to know why, the tighter the strangle. Fun fact: It's impossible to hold onto faith when you're chasing the need to know why. Yet I couldn't shake the lie that if only I knew why, I'd be able to accept it.

I was a devoted wife and stay-at-home mom for seventeen years. A real supermom (and by this I mean crazy). I made baby food from scratch and breastfed until my kids could pour their own milk. And my husband? He was super, too. He read every parent book written for fathers and covered every sharp corner and outlet. He never thought twice about being asked to run out for nipple pads, and when I expressed my fear of our baby being killed by the standing lamp, within minutes he had drilled it to the hardwood floor. I wrote, produced, and choreographed an original musical number for every daily mom-and-baby activity: a song for diaper changing, a song for nap time, a song for feeding time … you get the picture. And when I wasn't singing, we played the overpriced Baby Mozart CD we purchased back in the late

'90s, because it guaranteed that our kid would be a genius. I threw the best birthday parties in town, joined the Mom's Club, and took the kids to church every Sunday, despite the fact that wrangling an alligator in the pews fully naked would have been safer, easier, and less embarrassing. We read every baby book cover to cover and did exactly what the pediatrician told us to do. We enrolled our kids in Catholic school, despite not being able to afford it, and volunteered in the classroom. My husband coached them in sports, I organized weekly arts and crafts at the kitchen table, and on Friday nights, we made homemade pizzas and watched Disney movies, snuggled together on the couch. We weren't perfect, and if we could go back and change a few things, you can bet that we would. But on paper? We did everything right.

So when addiction threatened to destroy our family, all I could think was, *Lord, why? I did everything right. Why is everything so wrong?* It made no sense. As my confusion escalated, my faith plummeted. I became angry at God.

If you've ever struggled with loving a person who's been hijacked by addiction, you understand the great lengths and drastic measures people will take, all in the name of love, all in the hope of fixing and saving and bringing your loved one back home. We know no other way to survive this. Can I just say that the cross of addiction stinks? Honestly, there's no other way to describe it. But what made my cross even worse was believing that it was up to me to do the fixing, saving, and leading back home. I was terrified of surrendering and fully believing that God was in control, because … what if he wasn't? What if his plan wasn't to fix or save or bring back home? What if God's will didn't match mine? And so, I continued to dance around this cross, relying on my own will, my own love, to do the rescuing.

Despite being told at our first support group, "If our love could save our children, none of us would be here," I continued to grasp my ungodly self-reliance, believing that my love was different. And while my husband never voiced it, I think he secretly hoped that was true. If only protecting our most precious ones was as easy as dad nailing the lamp to the floor.

We tend to believe that when people are slammed with hard suffering, it's the pain of the trial that causes them to lose faith. But according to Dr. James Dobson, that's not true. He says that suffering isn't what shreds a person's faith. In fact, he believes that people have the ability to withstand an enormous amount of pain, provided the circumstances make sense. In other words, if we could just understand why the Lord has permitted us to suffer this or that, we'd accept it.

But would we really?

Something tells me that if God spoke to me right now and laid out all the reasons why he's allowed horrible things to happen in my life, I wouldn't be satisfied with his answer. I'd continue to doubt and question his motives. In theory, Jesus' death on the cross is enough; and when life is smooth sailing, it's more than enough. But when God sends trials and tribulations, the crucifixion becomes less real, less a part of my life, and I don't care to remember why Jesus suffered for me. I only want to understand why I have to suffer for him.

In his podcast *Gospel in Life*, Timothy Keller addresses two responses to our question "why," noting that both responses are wrong. The first response, says Keller, is the religious response, otherwise known as moralism. When we respond to suffering this way, we think we need to pray more or do more to receive God's blessing. We tell ourselves that God has punished us because we haven't been good enough. So we add more novenas to our prayer routine, put in time before the Blessed Sacrament, join another ministry or two, and vow to drop a few more dollars in the collection basket. We believe that the more we do for God, the less we'll suffer.

The second response to why we suffer is a secular response.

Everything that happens is erratic or aimless, and life is random. Suffering proves that there is no God, and that if there is, he's incompetent or indifferent. People with this response will tell you that God has no real control and probably doesn't even care about us that much. If God really loved us, he would never allow things like murder, disease, disaster, abuse, poverty, homelessness, and indoor water parks. This is the response of cynicism.

I know a great cynic, and his name is Satan. He stepped into our story at the very beginning, approaching Adam and Eve and convincing them that God didn't really love them. "Did God say, 'You shall not eat of any tree of the garden?'" (Gn 3:1). When Eve explains that God told them they could enjoy any fruit from any tree except for one tree, Satan the Cynic challenges her. He ever so subtly instills doubt in her mind: "You will not die. For God knows that when you eat of it your eyes will be opened, and you will be like God, knowing good and evil." In other words, "You idiot. Are you really buying that? That is not true. God is holding out on you. He doesn't want you to be wise like him — that's the real reason he forbade you to eat from the tree. So you see, he can't really be trusted and he must not be that good, or else he would let you eat whatever you wanted."

Eve's greatest mistake was not taking a bite out of the apple, but engaging in a conversation with the devil. That, my friends, is a conversation we stand no chance of winning. Once in conversation, the serpent tempts our first parents by stirring up confusion and doubt, leading them into sin and its devastating consequences. As the *Catechism* points out, that was the tragic day when mankind lost its trust that God's ways are ordered to our happiness (see 397).

The enemy of our souls has the same motive today that he had in that garden. He has not changed, nor is he original. He continues to use the same gameplay over and over again on us, and we continue to fall for it. How can we know when the drama of the first sin is playing out in our life? It happens every time we question God and his promises or doubt that his commands are given out of anything other than love for us.

Keller calls both the religious and the secular response spiritual dead ends. Having hit these dead ends myself, I have to agree. There's only one response to suffering that works, and it's taken me forty years to discover, and another five years to accept. It starts with remembering who God is. *God is love.* He has promised us, his beloved sons and daughters, that we will have to endure many trials in this life. He tells us that our hardships are necessary if we want to enter the kingdom of God (see Acts 14:22). Jesus told his followers plainly, "In the world you have tribulation; but be of good cheer, I have overcome the world" (Jn 16:33). This isn't hyperbole; it's a promise. A promise that assures us that whatever it is we're asked to suffer in this present time doesn't compare to the awesomeness that God has in store for us (Rom 8:18). And "We know that in everything God works for good with those who love him, who are called according to his purpose" (Rom 8:28).

If you were hoping for another way through the suffering you don't understand, be not afraid. We have a virtue we can apply to this cross and a mother who models it perfectly: lively faith.

### Mary's Lively Faith

Our Lady is the greatest example of embracing what God permits to happen without hesitation or looking to understand why. The *Catechism* tells us:

> The Virgin Mary most perfectly embodies the obedience of faith. By faith Mary welcomes the tidings and promise brought by the angel Gabriel, believing that "with God nothing will be impossible" and so giving her assent: "Behold I am the handmaid of the Lord; let it be [done] to me according to your word." Elizabeth greeted her: "Blessed

is she who believed that there would be a fulfillment of what was spoken to her from the Lord." It is for this faith that all generations have called Mary blessed. (148)

The moment I realized that the addiction festering beneath my roof was real, not immediately going away, and completely out of my control, I had two choices: I could accept it and live in the solution, or I could refuse it and remain living in the problem. This cross felt awful, painful, terrifying, and 100 percent not in my plan. I didn't even want to hear what God had to say about it. The longer I refused to receive what the Lord was offering me, searching for ways of comfort and relief outside of the cross, the heavier and more bitter my cross became.

Mary didn't resist the cross. Mary didn't hesitate. In her pure faith, Mary said "yes" to God's will, and she didn't ask why. St. Catherine of Siena offers us a beautiful reflection on self-knowledge; this is key to our understanding of Mary's faith:

Self-knowledge is the dwelling in which we discover our own lowliness, and this makes us humble. There we find the knowledge of God's goodness too, and in this light a warmth, a fire of love, is born in us — so gently that all bitterness becomes sweet, everything weak grows strong, and all the ice of selfish love melts away. We no longer love ourselves selfishly, but for God. And more, we pour out a river of tears and spread our loving desires out over all our sisters and brothers, loving them with a pure love, without self-interest. And we love God for God's sake, because he is supreme eternal Goodness, worthy of being loved.

Mary knew herself. She recognized her lowliness. She was certain of who God was, and who she was in relation to him. This is key.

(You might want to underline it.) Because of her self-knowledge, Mary was able to put her own will aside, accepting God's will instead. It's only in this holy dwelling of self-knowledge that Mary could love God for God's sake, performing all her actions out of this motive of pure love. Mary believed. Her faith didn't waver in the face of the impossible, the unpredictable, or the uncertain.

My faith is solid like Mary's — when life is smooth sailing and I'm holding a coconut milk latte. But when I hit a rough patch or when disappointment comes my way, I'm immediately sucked back into doubt and questioning God. It's like I have faith amnesia. Following Christ can be so frustrating.

And perhaps this is just one of the reasons why God permits suffering to intersect our lives. Our suffering can reveal things about us, like disordered attachments, unhealthy dependency, or anything that isn't from God, yet dominates our life. Small sins, when fertilized by disbelief and a lack of love, have the potential to grow bigger than our trial. Don't get me wrong: The hardships that we face aren't the cause of our sin, nor are our sufferings punishment for our sins. However, the trials of life can magnify the sins that were already there. And when we pay close attention to this — when we look inward and discover the evil that runs straight down the center of our hearts — we enter into the holy dwelling of self-knowledge. Here in this space, we discover our lowliness. Selfish love melts away, and we experience pure love for God — a love so pure that there is no longer any self-interest; we love God for God's sake and nothing else. This, my friend, is a lively faith.

We can know we're operating out of a lively faith when we lose our "why" and echo Mary's "how": "How can this be, since I have no husband?" (Lk 1:34). According to the Ignatius Catholic Study Bible, "Mary is not questioning God's ability to give her a son, but she is asking how such a plan will unfold. Her question, unlike Zechariah's question, 'How shall I know this?' (Lk 1:18) proceeds from faith and seeks to understand God's action, not to doubt it."

When I learned to replace my "why" with Mary's "how," my view of my cross changed. The Spirit broke through my scattered brain, shedding just enough light on the true meaning of love. Before this breakthrough, I despised the idea of "tough love." Tough love told me and my husband to detach with love. What did this look like for us? It looked like refusing to give our own son any money, or even a home, until there was an agreement for treatment — even if that meant missing Thanksgiving or Christmas or a birthday. This is hands down the most unnatural, gut-wrenching experience ever. It feels like the exact opposite of love, especially parental love. What kind of parent would allow their child to suffer? How can this possibly be love? This was a sharp sword aiming straight for my heart, and I did my best to dodge it. But then I looked at Mary, whose own heart was pierced by this sword. Mary allowed Jesus his suffering on the cross. Not only did she allow it, she participated in it. After all, it was by way of Mary that Jesus began his public miracles.

St. Louis de Montfort writes, "At the marriage of Cana He changed water into wine, but it was at Mary's humble prayer; and this was His first miracle of nature. He began and continued His miracles by Mary, and He will continue them to the end of ages by Mary." Pure love of God gave Mary the heavenly strength to love her own Son to the cross. It was Mary's tough love, her complete denial of her own self-interest, her own plan, her own feelings, that allowed lowly sinners like you and me to obtain eternal life.

And isn't this the greatest condition of discipleship? "If any man would come after me, let him deny himself and take up his cross daily and follow me" (Lk 9:23). We miss the point of this familiar verse because it's just that: familiar. So let's break it down, starting with *Come after me.* Can you see the Lord's eyes looking straight into your own as he commands this of you? Because he's speaking to you. This isn't a thoughtless suggestion or casual invitation to skip along behind Jesus. He's calling you to pursue him.

To hunt him down. This is what following Jesus looks like.

And if you're up to the pursuit, then you must *deny yourself.* What does this look like? Well, it looks like self-denial. Like saying "no" to yourself, no matter how right you think you are, and saying "yes" to God, no matter how wrong you feel he is. It means laying down everything within you that gives you a false sense of control, and handing yourself over to God, admitting you are a weak and powerless mess. In my case? Denying myself meant doing the opposite of what I wanted to do, for the sake of love.

Finally, we're told to *take up our cross daily and follow.* What marks the life of a true Christian is his cross and the way he carries it, not once in a lifetime, but daily. The cross is unavoidable, and no matter how hard you try to hide from it, it will find you. I know this for a fact. I have hidden to no avail, and yet my cross remains. But with Mary's example, relentless prayer, and a whole lot of tears, I've come to recognize that a love that only serves my interest isn't loving at all. Sometimes, love hurts.

Why is tough love so tough? Because it requires denying what you want for yourself and allowing God to do what *he* wants for you. For me, picking up the cross and following Jesus means denying my natural maternal instincts to protect, clean up, and keep safe. This is why I look to Mary. Mary trusted God and so she loved the cross. It sounds crazy, but she did: from the moment she said yes to God's plan, to the terrible moment when she stood at the foot of the cross as Jesus died. Imitating Mary's lively faith means trying to say yes like Mary. To live out of a faith like Mary's. To love God for God, like Mary. It isn't easy. None of this is. But it's worth it.

Just look up at the cross. Was that worth it? If you're not certain, ask the mother who is standing by it, pressing into her dying Son, meeting him in his suffering. If we aim to have a lively faith like Mary, we need to love like Mary. And the only way we learn this is by way of suffering. This means we must stop asking God *why* and ask to better understand *how.*

St. Louis de Montfort assures us:

> The more then, that you gain the favor of that August Princess and faithful Virgin, the more you will act by pure faith; a pure faith which will make you care hardly at all about sensible consolations and extraordinary favors; a lively faith animated by charity, which will enable you to perform all your actions from the motive of pure love; a faith firm and immovable as a rock, through which you will rest quiet and constant in the midst of storms and hurricanes, a faith active and piercing, which like a mysterious pass-key, will give you entrance into all the mysteries of Jesus, into the last ends of man, and into the heart of God himself; a courageous faith, which will enable you to undertake and carry out without hesitation great things for God and for salvation of souls.

A lively faith doesn't indicate an absence of storms, dear friend. It's what keeps us standing in the midst of them.

— 3 —

# Embracing Your Cross with Ardent Charity

✝

W hen I was young, I loved a lot of things: gymnastics, fried chicken and mashed potatoes, late nights at the Ardsley swim club, roller skating, and Kirk Cameron. I loved making ribbon barrettes. I loved going to Carvel for chocolate malts with my dad and Bloomingdale's for Guess jeans with my mom. I loved being on stage, sleepaway camp, and doing cartwheels on the beach. Can you think back to when you were young and recall the things that you loved?

As the years went on, I changed. The things that I loved changed, too (except for Kirk Cameron — I still love him). As a young adult, I discovered an insatiable desire to feel in love and to receive love. It sounds selfish, and that's because I *am* selfish. But then I had a baby. And all that love I desired for myself drained out of my pores and onto him.

From the moment my sweet baby boy was placed on my chest, love would never be the same. When his eyes met mine for the very first time, I made a vow to him: *I will never let anything happen to you. I will never let anyone hurt you. I will protect you and save you and keep you from harm.* Basically, the first thing I did to my child was lie. But at the time, I meant it. I believed that the burning, uncontainable love I held in my heart for this child was that powerful. In the moments after a woman gives birth, something happens. Like female elephants, our bonding hormones surge, and the instinct to protect our family kicks in. The day before I had my firstborn, I would have been prone to run from danger. But once this little life was placed in my arms, fleeing was no longer an option. This mama bear was staying put. There was nothing that I wouldn't do for him because of this love.

They say that a person in love will do unreasonable things for the beloved. My love surpassed unreasonable. My love bordered on crazy.

I remember the first time I heard the term "helicopter parent." First recorded in Dr. Haim Ginott's 1969 book *Between Parent & Teenager*, it's a term that was created by teens who said that their parents would hover over them like a helicopter. I believed that this is what a mother's love looks like: making sure you always know where your kid is and what he's doing and that he's safe and happy. In fact, the one thing I remember from all those well-visits to the pediatrician was how she'd write and circle the word SAFE-TY at the bottom of a little slip of paper, like a prescription. She'd hand it to me and send me off with my baby, reminding me, "If you do nothing else, keep him safe. That's your job."

What a stupid thing to say. I'm not implying that safety is a non-issue and that we should let our kids run wild with lollipops in their mouths, unattended and barefoot while holding scissors.

But it's untrue that it's all up to me — or my husband — to ensure my children's safety. Babies grow up, and no matter what we do, say, or teach, no matter how much we love, we're not responsible for our children's dwelling in safety. We can buckle them, pad them, helmet them, vaccinate them, quarantine them, sanitize them, mask them, homeschool them, medicate them — heck, we can bubble wrap them if we so desire, but we can never guarantee their safety. In fact, Scripture makes this clear in Psalm 4:8, "In peace I will both lie down and sleep; / for you alone, O LORD, make me dwell in safety." Safety is the Lord's job, not ours. My pediatrician left that part out, leading me to believe that my child's security and happiness was all up to me. At the time, it made perfect sense. After all, no one loved my child more than I did. He was my everything, and there was nothing I wouldn't do for him.

In the year following the Sandy Hook shooting, the Lord was preparing to teach me a great lesson — one that I resisted and abhorred at the time, but that I'd draw from for years to come. It was in this season of suffering that I was invited to participate in *his* kind of love, a suffering love, a pure love; a love that's not driven by feelings, but is rooted in desiring the greater good for another. In theory, this shouldn't be hard. Isn't this what we all want for those we love? Yet this proves difficult for most of us. Because the greater good is not always convenient or popular, and more often than not, it involves suffering. This is what the Lord was about to teach me: Sometimes the greater good means removing the safety net and letting our loved ones fall.

Luke, six years old at the time, was overcome by fear. To be fair, Luke was afraid before the shooting. He wasn't the kid who enjoyed the gory, scary element of Halloween, and Scooby Doo gave him nightmares (for obvious reasons — *the Creeper*). We had developed a bedtime routine of getting into Luke's bed with him, reading his favorite book, *The Action Bible*, and remaining there until he fell fast asleep. Then we'd roll to the side of the bed, silently slip to the ground, and crawl out of his room, praying that he didn't wake up. On a good night, Luke wouldn't get out of his bed for at least a couple of hours. But most nights it was just minutes later that he'd come tearing down the hallway, running into our bedroom, screaming, "I'm scared!" And so I'd scoop him up and wrap him tightly in my arms, allowing him to peacefully sleep in bed with me until morning. I say "with me" because Luke liked to sleep on a diagonal, kicking my husband throughout the night. Nick would eventually grab his pillow and go sleep in Luke's twin bed. We knew this wasn't great for our marriage, but you know what? Luke was my fourth kid, and by that stage of life, I wanted to sleep a whole lot more than I wanted to be married. That said, we'd agreed on a plan: After Christmas, we would be training Luke to stay in his own bed. No matter what.

Then December 14, 2012, happened.

As Luke's fear escalated after the shooting, my emotional capacity to handle anything plummeted. And those bedtime battles were, simply put, not worth fighting. More than being too exhausted and traumatized to deal with it, I didn't see anything wrong with it. The poor child had experienced the unimaginable. If he needed the comfort of his mother throughout the night, then that's what he'd get. Did this mean I had to sacrifice my own sleep? Sometimes. Did this add stress to my marriage? You bet. But isn't this what love is about? Isn't this what love does?

Therapy became the new normal for our Sandy Hook kids. That, and petting dogs and painting bells. We'd tried various therapists around town, but nothing seemed to work for Luke. His behavior was off the wall, and mindfulness, deep breathing, drawing stop signs, and collecting rubber ducks were all Band-Aids® for a deeper wound that required greater attention. Look, nobody likes their wounds poked at, because it hurts. We'd rather bandage them, cover them up so we can't see them. The problem is, you don't have to see your wound to feel it. We really wanted to heal Luke's wounds. So we put down the paint brushes and rubber ducks and headed for the best of the best: Yale Children's Trauma Clinic in New Haven, Connecticut, where we met Chris, who was completing his Fellowship in Psychology. The focus of his study was in trauma and anxiety interventions for adolescents, with research interest in gender socialization of boys. He was learned in the emotional expression and response following significant life events.

Finding Chris was like finding a buried treasure. He was exactly what Luke needed, and we all grew to adore him. He was a tall, thin young man, and very likable. With his granola vibe, always sporting a fleece vest and khakis, I imagined that when he wasn't at the office, he was backpacking in the mountains with a golden retriever by his side (because you know how New Haven is full of mountains). He was sincere and intelligent, and you could tell that he loved his work. He had a good sense of humor, which I always appreciate, was a great listener and teacher, and he genuinely cared for Luke. We met with Chris once a week for a full year, making the forty-five-minute trek to New Haven and back. It was hard work for Luke, but worth every minute. We love Chris and are forever indebted to him, because he gave our six-year-old boy his life back. How? By poking at the wound.

As much as I love Chris, though, I'll be honest: Most weeks I left his office hating him. You see, Chris asked us to do things that didn't feel like love and that went against my maternal instinct. Among other things, he told me to stop allowing Luke access to our bed. His theory was that while, in the moment, we felt like we were helping our son through his fear, ultimately, we were prolonging it, getting in the way of what's required to build up a boy's self-esteem, sense of worth, and confidence. Chris believed that our coddling Luke was preventing him from moving forward, keeping him from growing into the young man he was created to be. I wanted to pull Chris's stupid fleece vest tight around his neck and choke him to death, because obviously he had no idea what he was talking about. He had no kids! He wasn't even married yet! How could he possibly know what was good for my son? How could he so flippantly dismiss what my gut was telling me? What gave him the authority over my mama bear instinct? I remember thinking that if he could only see and hear my baby shaking, crying, and unable to breathe from fear, he'd understand that his plan was stupid, unhelpful, and borderline abusive.

But his plan worked.

Enduring my child's suffering was so difficult because I thought *I* was his savior. I believed, like the pediatrician told me, that it was my job to keep him happy and safe, and that I knew what was best for him. I thought the remedy and cure for his fear would come from me and my love. In truth, I'd made my children idols, with Motherhood as my identity. If my kids were happy, I was a good mom. If they depended on me for everything, that meant I was doing my job well. Everything I did, I did for the love of my children. And love is love, right? And while that sounds selfless and sweet and looks so good on a bumper sticker, that was the problem. We're supposed to do everything out of love for the Lord, not love for ourselves or even our children. The greatest commandment is not "You shall love your children with all your heart, and with all your soul, and with all your mind" but "You shall love the LORD your God with all your heart, and with all your soul, and with all your mind" (Mt 22:37).

Sometimes loving the Lord isn't so easy. Sometimes, what he asks us to do and endure for his sake feels too hard. Loving Luke — real love, as in desiring the greater good for him — through his fear required that I do the exact opposite of what my elephant instinct told me to do. It meant I had to let go of the need to step in when things got uncomfortable and allow God to show up and fill in the gap. Honestly, not allowing Luke to come into our bed for comfort felt like jumping out of an airplane without a parachute (which, for the record, is not on my bucket list). This was a cross I resisted taking hold of, and yet it's a cross I'm most grateful for, because what it has taught me has proven necessary over and over again.

To embrace crosses like this, we need Mary's virtue of ardent charity.

## Mary's Ardent Charity

Saint Anselm says, "Wherever there is the greatest purity, there is also the greatest charity." Whose heart was more pure than Mary's? As we've already noted, Mary, immaculately conceived, was humble and detached from earthly things. She was empty of self and full of God. She was asked to carry God's Son because she had the room to do so. Mary didn't love God because she was chosen. Mary was chosen because she loved God. She held nothing back from him, but gave him everything. This line from Song of Songs could have been the song of Mary's heart: "My beloved is mine and I am his" (2:16).

Saint Sophronius says, "Divine love so inflamed her, that nothing earthly could enter her affections; she was always burning with this heavenly flame, and, so to say, inebriated with it." Saint Ildephonsus said, "The Holy Ghost heated, inflamed, and melted Mary with love, as fire does iron; so that the flame of this Holy Spirit was seen, and nothing was felt but the fire of the love of God." St. Francis de Sales called Mary the "Queen of Love." Mary's heart was a burning flame of love that felt no burden and didn't fear the impossible, because with God there was no such thing. Mary lived in constant contemplation of the Lord, always pondering his workings in her life, performing all duties for love of him. It was this flame of love that inspired her to proclaim her great *fiat*, to set out in haste to visit Elizabeth, and to point out the needs of others at the wedding feast at Cana. Mary never looked at the gifts, but kept her eyes on the Giver. She knew the voice of her Lover and was eager to cooperate with his will and follow him anywhere, especially to the foot of the cross.

I didn't want to step back and allow my son to go through his suffering, but maybe not for the reason you think. Of course, I didn't want him to feel afraid or sad, or to think that I was abandoning him. I didn't want to have to hear him cry or see his tears or the fear on his face. I didn't want to have to untangle his arms from around my body. But mostly I didn't want to go through with this plan, because watching him suffer inevitably caused me suffering. I couldn't separate myself from him. Even though I knew this was for a greater good, the thought of having to participate in his pain, not prevent it, was unbearable. Still, I did it. I followed through with the plan. I grabbed my rosary beads, and I prayed my way through it. I asked Mama Mary to comfort Luke because I couldn't. And after a few brutal nights, Luke was sleeping soundly in his own bed. He wasn't scarred for life. He didn't think I'd abandoned him. In peace he lay down and slept, happy, confident, and unafraid.

How'd I do it? I wonder about that myself. In looking back on that season, I'm especially struck by a strength that wasn't my own. It's as if a piece of armor was placed upon me as I went into battle. The fact of the matter is, *I* didn't do it; it was the Holy Spirit.

We forget about the Holy Spirit, don't we? Most of us say we run to Jesus or God the Father, but how often do we call upon the Holy Spirit? Mary is a perfect model for remaining in and calling upon the Holy Spirit — after all, we call her the "Spouse of the Holy Spirit." That blew my mind the first time I read it. We read in the Gospel of Luke: "And the angel said to her, 'The Holy Spirit will come upon you, and the power of the Most High will overshadow you; therefore the child to be born will be called holy, the Son of God'" (Lk 1:35).

St. Louis de Montfort further explains:

God the Holy Ghost, being barren in God — that is to say not producing another Divine Person — is become fruitful by Mary, whom He has espoused. It was with her, in her and of her, that He produced His Masterpiece, which is God made Man, and that He goes on producing daily, to the end of the world, the predestinate and the members of the Body of that adorable Head. This is the reason why He, the Holy Ghost, the more He finds Mary, His dear and inseparable spouse, in any soul, the more active and mighty He becomes in producing Jesus Christ in that soul, and that soul in Jesus Christ.

Maybe you're thinking, "That's great for Mary, but I'm not espoused to the Holy Spirit. How can I ever love God the way that Mary does?" It's true, we're not married to the Holy Spirit. However, when Jesus ascended to heaven, he not only left us Mary as mother, but he also left us the Advocate — the Holy Spirit — to help us. This is the same Spirit that drives out demons, cleanses lepers, and raises the dead. Why aren't we inviting this Spirit into every second of our lives? If we want to imitate Mary's virtue of charity, we're going to need heavenly help, because charity is a theological virtue. We can't earn it or work for it, we can only ask God to give it to us and increase it in us.

This love that comes from God gives us the courage to do hard things. We may never understand how it's possible to love a God that allows us to watch our loved ones suffer. But if we can resist the need to understand and replace it with what we already know is true about God, our cross will begin to look more like a gift than a punishment. If this love — the kind that conquers all our fear — is what we desire, then we must invite the Blessed Mother into our hearts.

In consecrating myself to the Blessed Mother, I've discovered that Mary not only knows everything we're going through, but she's felt everything. When we feel like we're being asked to walk through the unimaginable, we need to reflect on Mary and her life with Jesus. We need to call on the Holy Spirit and ask him to do in us what we cannot do by our own strength. And we need to participate in the sacraments, taking full advantage of their power.

Mary loved Jesus more than anyone else ever can or will, and she not only allowed him to fall three times, but to stand back up, carry his own cross, and embrace it by being fastened to it. Not once did she leave his side or hide her eyes or demand that they take him down. She didn't flee in the face of danger, but stood by and willingly suffered with Jesus, by Jesus, and for Jesus, because she loved God and knew that he works all things for good for those who love him. She believed this to the point of her Son's death.

Our Blessed Mother is more than a sweet little girl who loved Jesus. Our Lady is a tower of ardent charity. When I'm feeling low on love, I run to Mary. I beg for her pure heart in exchange for my own. When I'm happy, I know that my heavenly mother rejoices with me. And when I'm faced with deep sorrow, who understands better than Mary? I love the example of St. Maximilian Kolbe, related to us by one of his religious brothers: "When things ... were going well, he rejoiced with all his heart with everyone and fervently thanked the Immaculata for the graces received through her intercession. When things went badly he was still happy and used to say, 'Why should we be sad? Doesn't the Immaculata, our little mother, know everything that's going on?'"

If you want your cross to be sweet, learn to love like Mary. It's in discovering this pure love that we are able to hear the promise that only God can make: *I will never let anything happen to you. I will never let anyone hurt you. I will protect you and save you and keep you from harm.*

— 4 —

# Embracing Your Cross with Unwavering Trust

✝

Ever notice the similarities between Mary at the Annunciation and Princess Jasmine in the Disney movie *Aladdin*? I'm thinking of that one scene when Aladdin, floating on the magic carpet, reaches out his hand to the princess, looks her in the eyes, and asks, "Do you trust me?" His invitation is risky and comes with no guarantee. I feel like this is what God did with Mary, and he does it with us, too. He appears out of nowhere, looks us in the eyes, and asks, "Do you trust me?" Saying yes to God's invitation is kind of like stepping off a balcony and onto a magic carpet. It's daring and uncertain, but ultimately, it's a beautiful ride with a new point of view.

I learned the importance of trust in a quiet church in Rhode

Island years ago.

It was early July, and my family (minus our oldest son who courageously agreed to sober living in California) was headed to Rhode Island for two days of much-needed rest. We aren't "that family" that vacations. Not in the summer. Not ever, really. Just the way the paycheck falls over here. After years of chaos, worry, and off-the-charts stress as our son saught treatment in another state, we were all finally afforded the opportunity to take a much-needed deep breath. So when a sister in Christ kindly offered her beach home to my family, we jumped at the offer, took out our calendars, and began searching for a chunk of time that was not already filled with work, cheerleading, and football practice. As we sat at the kitchen table staring at the weeks ahead, the reality of our day-to-day living hit us. The only day we could get away was *this* day — as in, the one that was already happening. If you think that Mary moved in haste, you should've seen us!

Annie and I made a quick run to Target, filling empty bags with bathing suits, beach cover-ups, boogie boards, flip-flops, sunblock, and snacks in record time. With just one hour to pack, arrange care for the pets, and hit the road, there was no time to waste. Back at the house, I got right to work, pulling dusty suitcases out of closets and fishing for old backpacks hidden under beds. Then my husband's phone rang. I've already told you how I feel about a ringing phone: immediate panic. I tried to weed the fear out of my mind by reminding myself that it's the phone's job to ring, and not all calls are bad news.

It was bad news.

The person on the other end of the phone was the manager of the sober living house. Apparently, when my son shared his plans to leave California earlier that week, he wasn't joking or trying to manipulate me. He was serious. He was ready to go and had already purchased a plane ticket back home. And just like that, calming thoughts of beach and sand were replaced with fearful thoughts of *What's next?*

Fear is amazing, isn't it? In a split second, the fear of an uncertain future completely hijacked the joy of the present moment. I allowed the unknown to unravel the known because, deep down, I didn't trust that God was in control. How could he be? After all, this wasn't the plan! We had a plan, Lord! Why did you have to go and screw it all up? I fought with my husband as he aggressively peeled out of the driveway too fast, because this, my friend, is what a superficial vision of God looks like. This is what happens when an obstacle lands in your well-laid out plans and you lack genuine trust in the Lord. It makes you speed, as if by driving too fast you can somehow move ahead of it.

By the time we arrived at the beach house, heightened emotion gave way to unrest — something that I was growing accustomed to living with. The house was just perfect, a few steps from the beach, with the distinct smell of salt in the air. We explored our temporary home, peeking inside cabinets, fishing bikes out of the shed, and choosing our bedrooms. As I made my way from room to room, Jesus was in the details. The entire house had been lovingly sprinkled with hope: a crucifix here, the Divine Mercy image there, a Scripture verse printed and hanging on the wall. And in the room that I chose for myself? Roses. Like a nod from Saint Thérèse and Our Lady ... these heavenly friends of mine had made certain to see to it that I wasn't alone. An even bigger God wink than the roses was St. Clare's Church that stood on the corner at the end of the street. I noticed it as we pulled onto the block, and made a mental note of what time daily Masses were offered. The ability to receive Jesus in the Eucharist was such a gift from God. I badly needed that storehouse of power.

The next morning, I walked to Mass alone (unless you count the anxiety I carried with me as a friend, because Lord knows it invites itself over as if it's my BFF). *What are you doing, Lord?* was all I could ask. And honestly, I didn't even care about his answer.

Not anymore. I was too disappointed. I know — it sounds terrible to say that I was upset that my son was returning home. It feels equally terrible to write. But make no mistake — I love him, and I wanted nothing more in this lifetime than to have my scattered family put back together. But the pieces of us were still very much broken. No amount of crazy glue could fix us. What we needed was more time. Time for us to process it all, and time for God to heal us. Months prior, I had given all my children to God by consecrating them to Jesus through Mary. I surrendered them ... but not completely. I was still holding the reins, afraid to let go. And so I just couldn't understand why, after so much work, so much promise, so much hope, so much money, the Lord would allow anything other than my will to happen.

There's something sweet about physically walking to Mass. I felt like I'd set out on a pilgrimage. I entered the church and breathed in the familiarity. There's nothing quite like our Universal Church. It's kind of like the mall, minus the noise. No matter what state you're in when you find it, you immediately feel at home. It's so rare in our world and everyday life to find quiet. So, when Mass was over, I remained in the pew. I got on my knees and leaned into the silence. I wanted to trust God. I wanted a genuine faith that didn't get tossed about by whatever was happening to me at that moment. But there I was, tossed about. I'd placed my hope in this plan of ours, not in God's will. The result was anxiety, discouragement, and waning trust.

There were no tears, no fist-shaking at the heavens. Nothing about my posture said, *this girl is in desperate need of something,* like that one time I dragged myself through the aisles of Target openly crying. (Yeah, that happened.) When I finished my prayer, I calmly sat back in the pew and started to collect my things. Then I became aware of a man one pew behind, standing over me. I turned to say hello, but he spoke before I could. "The Lord is going to take care of you," he assured me. In a matter of seconds, hundreds of thoughts ran through my mind. I wondered, *Do I look pathetic? Do I look like I need taking care of?* I thought I'd been looking pretty pulled together, considering everything going on. Why would he say that to me? I smiled and thanked him, not too sure what to make of this. I assumed he was probably just a lonely elderly man who does this — makes the rounds blessing everyone in his sight, bless his heart. But before I got up to leave, he looked me in the eyes and said six words that made me believe otherwise: "He told me to tell you."

I went back to the same Mass the next day, hoping to see this man. My mind couldn't rest. I had questions for him. Lots of questions. For starters, who are you? An angel? God's messenger? But more importantly, when you say, "The Lord will take care of you," what do you mean, exactly? In what way? Can you elaborate, please? I couldn't rest in the hope that this stranger freely offered me, in the name of Jesus. Nope. I needed to know more. I wanted specifics. Detailed information. Instead of rejoicing in God's message, I beat it to a pulp. What if this message meant, *This isn't going to go well, but don't worry, God will help you through*? Because that wasn't what I was praying for. That wasn't my idea of being taken care of. I wanted the Lord to take care of me by doing what I said. How could I possibly trust a God that I no longer believed knew what was best for me?

If there was ever a time I needed Mary's virtue of unwavering trust, it was in that sweet little church just a stone's throw from the beach.

## Mary's Unwavering Trust

Because of her unwavering trust, Mary could choose what God had planned for her life.

"Many of our problems with trust come because we don't understand the object of our trust," says Joseph A. Langford in his book *I Thirst: 40 Days with Mother Teresa*. "The object of trust is not the confidence that God will give, or do, or change, whatever we are asking of him. It is rather confidence in our union with him, the firm belief that whatever is happening now is the best that could happen to advance our union."

Don't brush by that too quickly. Go back and read it again. It's a gamechanger for those of us who struggle with trust. Langford goes on: "Rather than hoping in God and all that he wills, we can pin our hopes and desires on superficial things. Instead of hoping for God's presence and the fullness of what he has planned, we find ourselves only hoping for this or that immediate event or thing."

What I've realized about myself is that I want to understand why God so often doesn't cooperate with the plan I've given him. My problem is one of perspective, as I'm looking at things with surface vision. If I pulled back the lens and looked at life through God's eyes, making union with him my goal — then perhaps I too could obtain this virtue of unwavering trust in God and embrace what he has planned for me and allowed for good, even if I do not understand. To do this, I need to completely let go of control.

This is why I cling to Mary.

This is why we should all cling to Mary.

God didn't forget to include "how to carry" instructions with our cross, though we often think he did. Quite the contrary: It's directly from the cross that he gives us all the direction we need: "Behold your Mother." Mary, the "perfect mold of God," *is* our manual. Her *fiat* at the Annunciation was solid, never seeking to understand why, and she certainly didn't trouble herself the day after her encounter by searching for the messenger with a list of questions, beginning with, *Exactly what did you mean when you addressed me as full of grace?* Mary knew all that she needed to know about God from the Scriptures, and, because of that knowledge, she could trust him. We, too, can have this trust, if we listen to what God has to say about who he is, rather than what our clueless friends have to say about who they think he is.

Trusting in God's plan for my life is one thing. Trusting in his plan for my child's life gets a little trickier. Let's be honest, moms and dads. We have our own plans when it comes to our kids, don't we? We have all sorts of expectations and dreams, half of which we form before our children are even born. For instance, when my first son was born, my husband couldn't get him into his New York Yankees onesie fast enough! All his sports teams were picked out for him, and my husband patiently waited for the day that he and his "little buddy" could go out in the yard and toss a ball. Imagine the surprise then when his little buddy begged for The Wizard of Oz Barbie doll! Purchasing a Barbie for his son — which he did — was definitely not something my husband had planned for.

Before my first daughter was born, I knew exactly how I would dress her. She'd wear all pink with a bow in her hair until she was at least sixteen. Not once did I plan that she'd love to wear all black, pierce her nose, and tattoo a tiger's head pierced with a dagger … on her thigh. But lo and behold, she did! I am OK with it now, really. I let go of my hopes for the pink bow when she came home with a giant tattoo of a panther on her forearm. Here's the reality: My beautiful children belong to God and are on their own journey. God has a purpose for them that only they can fulfill. I have to trust that he's got them and resist the urge to bulldoze over him. In the grand scheme of things, a little boy with a Barbie and a teenage daughter with a tattoo aren't things to fear or worry about at all. It was facing a life touched by addiction that had me undone. This is what made me doubt God's promises and had me paralyzed by fear, because I didn't trust God enough to surrender to what he allowed in my life.

Mary, on the other hand, trusted in God's plan for her Son's life. And she put her full trust in Christ, too, fully believing that by following God's plan, she would spend a glorious eternity in his presence forever. Mary lived her life by the blueprint of Proverbs

3:5–6: "Trust in the Lord with all your heart, / and do not rely on your own insight. / In all your ways acknowledge him, / and he will make straight your paths." But let me make something clear here. Making our paths straight doesn't mean they'll be free of bumps and potholes. A straight path isn't the same as a smooth path, and making the decision to follow Christ doesn't automatically guarantee that these bumps go away. In fact, we're guaranteed the opposite. We're promised that this life will have its share of trouble. It's only when we open our heart to Jesus, relying on him and being mindful of him, that the roots of trust grow deeper. The straight path isn't one that's free of obstacles, but one whose obstacles we've learned to navigate around.

The words of that stranger in that sweet church in Rhode Island have stayed with me. Taking a cue from Mary, I continue to ponder them in my heart. The promise revealed to me continues to be fulfilled. The Lord *is* taking care of me. He's taking care of us all. And while we may never fully understand God's plan, we can find comfort in knowing that we don't have to. We're not called to understand, but we are called to trust. It's not my habitual response, but I'm working on it. I keep Mary close and meditate on her life often, seeking to imitate her unwavering trust. And I remind myself of Langford's words: "The more our trust resembles that of Our Lady, the more fully will we bring about this incarnation so longed for by the Lord. This is why there is so much power in making her response our own: 'Behold, I am the handmaid of the Lord; let it be to me according to your word' (Luke 1:38)."

— 5 —

# Embracing your Cross with Divine Wisdom

✝

If I had the money, I'd be a stress shopper. I could numb myself all day long at HomeGoods, Ikea, even the grocery store. And I don't think this is just a woman thing. You men do it, too. You might not buy shoes and home furnishings, but golf clubs, the latest electronics, another flat-screen TV, more football gear for your kid, another dog … or is my husband alone on this one?

There was a period when I chose to pick up my credit card in place of my cross, and it didn't end well. Turns out, retail therapy is a hoax, unless your idea of therapy is falling into financial and spiritual debt — then it's great. Thanks to God's grace (which is free), I climbed my way out of both debts. Now, we do grown-up things like budget, save, only buy what we need, and feel our pain

— most of the time.

I have a weakness for handmade rosaries and religious jewelry. I'm an Etsy small shop owner's dream, especially if I'm facing a season of suffering. I can justify this kind of retail therapy: It's religious, therefore it'll help. When I was working on accepting my son's substance abuse, I found the perfect necklace for it. (Bet you never thought about matching jewelry to your current suffering.) What caught my eye was a long, beaded necklace with a charm that reads: "God grant me the serenity to accept the things I cannot change, courage to change the things I can, and wisdom to know the difference."

The Serenity Prayer is one of the most well-known prayers of our time. Originally written by theologian Reinhold Niebuhr (although there is some controversy about whether Niebuhr is the author), it became widely popular when Alcoholics Anonymous (AA) adopted it as a part of its Twelve-Step program. As I wrestled with acceptance, I wore this necklace like armor and prayed that prayer daily. There was only one problem: *Wisdom*. I lacked it. And no one on Etsy was selling it. What even *is* wisdom?

I found this definition of wisdom at CatholicCulture.org:

> The first and highest gift of the Holy Spirit. It makes the soul responsive to God in the contemplation of divine things. Where faith is a simple knowledge of the articles of Christian belief, wisdom goes on to a certain divine penetration of the truths themselves. Built into wisdom is the element of love, which inspires contemplative reflection on these divine mysteries, rejoices dwelling on them and directs the mind to judge all things according to their principles.

I had to read this definition forty times before I sort of understood it.

I've always associated wisdom with intelligence. No wonder I struggled writing this chapter. I failed high school biology, I don't have a degree in theology, I used to crawl out of lectures in college (as in, I got on the floor and crawled out of class), and I can't even help my kid with eighth-grade math — because, can someone please tell me why we don't teach kids to carry the one anymore? That was the only part of my math class that I understood: Carrying the one. Why did we stop carrying it? So when I hear "wisdom," I immediately assume I don't have it. Wisdom is for smart people. It's too complicated for someone like me to comprehend. I'll never grasp the meaning of it. Yet true wisdom is a virtue; it's not about intelligence, but relationship.

St. Louis de Montfort writes about wisdom in his book *Love of the Eternal Wisdom*:

> Wisdom is better than strength and prudence is better than courage. Listen, therefore, kings, and understand. Learn, you judges of the nations ... desire ardently to know my words, love them and you will find instruction in them. ... Wisdom is resplendent and her beauty never fades. Those who love her will have no trouble in recognising her; and those who seek her will find her ... she goes around seeking those worthy of her, graciously shows her ways to them, guides them and provides for them with loving care.

Love. Seek. Beauty. Listen. Recognize. Find. Guide. Provide. Care.

Are these words you'd use to describe your intelligence? Or are these words you might use to describe a relationship?

Even after my reversion back to the Catholic Faith, my relationship with God was a real work in progress. It still is. Courting is a slow process, you know. True romance doesn't rush itself. Like a good cook, it knows that to achieve the best flavor, you need to let things simmer and marinate. True love goes beyond head knowledge, because head knowledge in a relationship will only get you so far. Memorizing the facts will help you only so much. If it's wisdom you're in search of, you need to get out of your head.

Have you ever lived in your head? It's a dark place, isn't it? I added years to my suffering because I lived in my head and believed every stupid thought I had. Do you ever think about what you think about? Dr. Caroline Leaf, a communication pathologist and cognitive neuroscientist, has researched the mind-brain connection, the nature of mental health, and the formation of memory, and she has this to say about our thoughts: "Thoughts are real, physical things that occupy mental real estate. Moment by moment, every day, you are changing the structure of your brain through your thinking. When we hope, it is an activity of the mind that changes the structure of our brain in a positive and normal direction."

The first time I read this, I was fascinated by how similar the scientific research of the mind is to Scripture. Scripture is full of references to the mind and our thoughts. Consider the popular verse Philippians 4:8: "Finally, brethren, whatever is true, whatever is honorable, whatever is just, whatever is pure, whatever is lovely, whatever is gracious, if there is any excellence, if there is anything worthy of praise, think about these things."

What do you think about?

When you go to bed, do you think about all the things on your to-do list that you didn't get to? Or do you recall all the things you did get done?

When you wake up, do you hit snooze, delaying the dreaded day ahead? Or do you roll out of bed and onto your knees, beginning your day in thanksgiving?

Are your thoughts stuck in the past, dragging you down the path of shame and regret? Or do you stay in the present moment, trusting that God knows what he's doing and that his plan for you is good?

If our thoughts precede our actions, and hope can change the structure of our brain, then mindset is everything. Romans 12:2 instructs us: "Do not be conformed to this world but be transformed by the renewal of your mind, that you may prove what is the will of God, what is good and acceptable and perfect." In other words, think differently. Think with the mind of Christ. Keep your thoughts holy so your actions will be holy, and in doing so, you'll be able to recognize God's will for your life.

Our minds are so powerful, running twenty-four hours a day. We think nonstop. I can pray the Rosary, plan dinner, and worry about everything all at the same time. And don't get me started on how well I can focus on what might happen someday (which, for the record, is never good). The more we focus on something, the more that something controls us. And knowing this, the enemy works overtime, blinding our minds because he understands that if he can keep our minds in the dark, we'll never be able to put on the mind of Christ and see the light of the Gospel (see 2 Cor 4:3–5).

While renewing our minds sounds great in theory, practically speaking, how do we do this? It's quite simple. We need to ardently desire Divine Wisdom, seeking access to God's goodness. Simple? Yes. Easy? Not so much. As we read in Scripture, "Wisdom is radiant and unfading, / and she is easily discerned by those who love her, / and is found by those who seek her" (Wis 6:12). "Our capacity to access God's goodness," says Dr. Leaf, "is based upon our wisdom, and wisdom comes from spending time in the Word of God." Does this remind you of anyone?

## Mary's Divine Wisdom

Mary, who spent time in the Word, was also the one in whom the Divine and Eternal Word lived. Does reading this make you feel like your head might explode? Saint Maximilian Kolbe can help us:

What type of union is this [between the Holy Spirit and Mary]? It is above all an interior union, a union of her essence with the essence of the Holy Spirit. The Holy Spirit dwells in her, lives in her. This was true from the first instant of her existence. It was always true, it will always be true.

In what does this life of the Spirit in Mary consist? He himself is uncreated Love in her; the Love of the Father and the Son, the Love by which God himself loves himself, the very love of the most Holy Trinity. He is a fruitful Love, a "Conception." Among creatures made in God's image the union brought about by married love is the most intimate of all (see Mt 19:6). In a much more precise, more interior, more essential manner, the Holy Spirit lives in the soul of the Immaculata, in the depths of her very being. He makes her fruitful from the very first instant of her existence, all during her life, and for all eternity.

I remember the first time it was pointed out to me that Mary stood at the foot of the cross. For years I'd imagined her lamenting on the ground. I can't imagine anything worse than witnessing the murder of your child. Wouldn't you do anything and everything in your power to protect him, stop it, pull him down from the cross? How could she stand and watch? I had to look away when I took my daughter for a COVID test! So how did Mary do it? It was the grace of heavenly (or divine) wisdom. Wisdom gave Mary the strength to do the will of God. It's this same divine wisdom that also gives you and me the strength and faith to submit to God's will.

Yes, Mary didn't have original sin, and it's easy to assume this means we can never be like her, so our poor choices and harmful decisions are justified. Yet the story of the Annunciation points out that Mary and we have some basic human things in common. Things like hearing what God wants us to do and feeling afraid. How do we know she was afraid? Because when the angel appeared, he said, "Do not be afraid." And after that, something noteworthy happens. As Father Cameron explains, "Why were the angel's words to be trusted? Because when Gabriel said to Mary, 'Do not be afraid' (Luke 1:30), she stopped being afraid. The Word of God transfigured her. What the angel announced to her corresponded with the deepest longings of her humanity."

We too need to be transfigured by the Word of God. For this to happen, we must seek silence and invite the Holy Spirit in. This starts by praying through Scripture. Not just reading or studying it, but praying with it, meditating on a verse or word, and losing ourselves in God's story. To reach this level of interior union, we need to empty ourselves of our idea of God, while maintaining an open and trusting attitude of the soul. We need to pay attention to our motive. Are we going into prayer as a means to get to God, or to get something from God? When we carve out intentional time and sit with God's Word, we enter into what is known as passive prayer — a prayer that God does in us. This is the prayer that transforms our life and sanctifies our soul, changing our vision. We begin to see with God's eyes, hear with God's ears, and think with God's mind.

Submitting ourselves to the will of God and asking him to transform our thoughts into his own is the secular world's nightmare. The world encourages us to think for ourselves, find our own truth, and never let anyone choose what is best for us. But what about when we find ourselves truly uncertain? Father Cameron points out that Mary, confronted by an impossible plan, didn't focus on the problem of it, but on the God who was behind it. He goes on:

> For faith is not something that I think up; it is not the fruit of analysis. Neither does faith equal "keeping rules": It is

not the result of my initiatives to get close to God; it is not the outcome of my "ethical excellence." Faith is a response to something that happens outside of me. Faith entails acknowledging an exceptional presence that chooses to come to me — a presence that radically changes my life, infusing it with an intensity and fullness I cannot bring about on my own.

I was recently asked, "When did you feel the Word of God working in your life?" and I struggled to answer. I was combing the archives of my brain for that moment the skies opened and the earth quaked, where suddenly I was glowing like lightning in a robe white as snow. But my relationship with the Lord hasn't been that way. More prone to resist God's will than I am to embrace it, my faith journey has played out more like a Paula Adbul song than the Resurrection story: one step forward, two steps back. Sure, there are those days when a word or verse jumps out of my Bible and slaps me in the face, and happiness swells that I cannot explain. But most of the time it's not a singular moment of grace, but a series of grace-filled moments carefully strung together. In a sense, my life has been one little Annunciation after another — always an opportunity for fear, followed by the invitation to say yes.

The less I turn to people, social media, and the world to solve my life's problems, and the more I turn to God's Word for answers, the more at peace I am. As we are instructed in Proverbs 2:1–11:

My son, if you receive my words
    and treasure up my commandments with you,
making your ear attentive to wisdom
    and inclining your heart to understanding;
yes, if you cry out for insight
    and raise your voice for understanding,

if you seek it like silver,
   and search for it as for hidden treasures;
then you will understand the fear of the LORD
   and find the knowledge of God.
For the LORD gives wisdom;
   from his mouth come knowledge and understanding;
he stores up sound wisdom for the upright;
   he is a shield to those who walk in integrity,
guarding the paths of justice
   and preserving the way of his saints.
Then you will understand righteousness and justice
   and equity, every good path;
for wisdom will come into your heart,
   and knowledge will be pleasant to your soul;
discretion will watch over you;
   understanding will guard you.

As we learn from Solomon, the clarity of mind and heart we gain from wisdom is far more important than anything else in the world. It's an intimate relationship with the Lord, yet how many of us order life this way?

It's the age-old response to suffering, and I've seen it played out firsthand in my own community. When tragedy strikes, there are only two options: walk toward God or walk away. When we insist on seeking a life without the cross, we walk away. The danger we run into when we fail to enter into a personal relationship with the Lord is that we become like the lost sheep we hear of in the parable, or the people invited to the banquet who find every reason under the sun not to attend. The world is full of lost sheep and people too busy to RSVP. More of us wander away from the feast, rather than enter into it.

On his *Word on Fire* show, Bishop Robert Barron reminds us that "the wines and food laid out at the banquet in Proverbs is

God's own flesh and that Wisdom wants us to feed on his very self." He also says, "Once you have this wisdom, it is hard to let go, for without wisdom we won't know what to do with the goods of the world — they'll eventually turn on us. But with wisdom, we will know how to use and enjoy even the simplest things that we have, and they will enhance our lives, thirty, sixty, one hundred-fold."

One of our Lady's many titles is "Seat of Wisdom." Jesus, Eternal Wisdom and Word of God, dwelt in her, was cradled in her arms, and rested safely on her lap. Mary, in a sense, is the human throne of him who reigns in heaven. Divine Wisdom cultivated a desire deep within herself for all that is beyond this world. Her gaze was upward, and every moment of her life was spent seeking God, finding God, and loving him above all things. This is what allowed her to embrace the cross. Accepting a share of Christ's suffering is what entering into a relationship with Jesus is. As St. Louis de Montfort says, "Wisdom is the Cross and the Cross is Wisdom."

We'll all endure times of weakness and wandering. When we find ourselves here, let's look to find Mary. Like John at the foot of the cross, let's seek out our mother and stand with her. She'll remind us that there's so much more to our story than what we can see, not by pulling us away from our cross, but by encouraging us to lean into it. This is what Mary does for us. And when we grab a hold of our cross in this way, we can accept the things we cannot change, find the courage to change the things we can, and have the wisdom to know the difference. A treasure, indeed.

— 6 —

# Embracing Your Cross with Heroic Patience

✝

Every summer when I was a kid, we'd all pile into the back of the station wagon to make the two-day, no-end-in-sight drive from Ardsley, New York, to Hilton Head Island, South Carolina. There were no seatbelts, no technology, and no endless supply of snacks. We learned how to entertain ourselves by leafing through books, looking out of car windows, and searching for the alphabet on highway signs and license plates. And every ten minutes or so, we inevitably asked, "Are we almost there yet?"

The two-day road trip in the back of the Buick holds a volume of stories we never would've had access to had we taken a quicker route. The way that my sister would sink low into the seat and move her legs up in the air, as if she were walking on the car's ceiling. The bathroom breaks and dirty rest stops where we encountered all sorts of humanity and my father's constant reminder to "wash your hands!" The excitement over my dad's CB radio purchase and laughing at his handle, "Kermit the frog." The Waffle House restaurant on every corner and how hysterical we thought we were, shouting, "Waffle House! I haven't seen one of those in a long time!" The tease and temptation of the countless South of the Border billboards, with each graphic and one-liner more stupid than the next, that led us to crushing disappointment when we arrived and realized that it was a total dump! The way my dad would ask for a shoulder rub as the hours got long, and how I loved to nestle my head on a pillow propped up against the window, watching the headlights glow while the sky grew dark. And while I'm sure there was complaining and fighting and inevitable restlessness, when my family gathers today and we reflect on these trips, there's nothing but laughter. There was something sweet about that long and endless road. We were a station wagon fueled by anticipation, rolling down I-95 to the tune of John Denver, longing for the southern sand and sun that was waiting to greet us.

Forty-plus years have passed since those family road trip days, and only now have I recognized the lesson the Lord was teaching me in the back of that Buick: the beauty and importance of patience. I look back on those trips and feel a longing for a life that is simple and unrushed — because is it just me, or does every day feel like a fire drill? Does every minute need to be one of entertainment? I try to imagine my own crew of kids stuffed into a car with no internet for two whole days, and honestly, I don't think they could do it. I don't think they could even do it *with* the internet, because, you know, the internet sometimes goes out, and if you've ever lived with a teenager when the internet goes out, you know exactly what I am talking about. When iPhone chargers go missing, Wi-Fi is lost, and batteries die, you might as well have run out of oxygen. No one knows how to be bored anymore, and patience is a thing of the past. The days of looking out a car window and being okay with that are over.

As I sat down to write this chapter, we were nearing the nine-month marker of the most unusual, unprecedented time in our lives: the Coronavirus Pandemic. This deadly virus felt like a marathon without a finish line. I was fine the first few weeks, almost giddy at the idea of God hitting the pause button so that I could deep clean closets, take long walks with the dogs, and play card games with the kids. But as life shut down, this permission to rest quickly changed from welcome to challenging. The race officially went too long. "Two weeks to slow the spread" turned into "Well, who knows?" and for most folks, that didn't sit too well. The uncertainty of the future, mixed with fear, was brewing stronger than that third pot of coffee I shouldn't have made. And yet, here we all were, reaching for another cup of joe (because what else was there to do), wondering why we couldn't shake the queasiness and involuntary twitching. Like kids thrown into the back of a station wagon on an endless road, we all began to wonder, *Are we almost there yet?*

If there is one thing I learned about myself during the pandemic, it's that I love a good challenge. Speaking gigs canceled? I'll take them virtual! Bible study shut down? No worries, we can meet on Zoom! I refused to be taken down. But as weeks turned into months and months to a year, my zeal to emerge strongly from the pandemic finally gave way to weariness. I might not have been taken down, but I was nearing a breakdown. The hope I had been preaching got buried somewhere beneath a pile of canceled plans and broken dreams. And my positive outlook? It might have taken its last breath at the announcement of no football for my son and the hybrid model for school. If that wasn't enough, the Lord sent a literal hurricane our way, shutting down our power and use of running water, all in the same month that my laptop died and my daughter crashed my new car. *Seriously, Lord*, I wondered. *To what end? Where are you? Why the delay? What is in store for my family, community, the world?* Life was beginning to feel stripped of every good thing, and the road we were on was bleak and headed for nowhere. At least I-95 had South of the Border billboards to look at!

And perhaps that was the greatest hurdle of all: the not knowing. We all have this desire to know the future — that urge to pick up the veil and take a peek. At the root of this desire is fear. We want to know how much longer, when will this end, and what will become of us, as if we'd be satisfied with the answer. As if knowing the date were the true remedy for the peace our hearts lack. These are the weeds, sprouted from seeds of fear, that thrive and grow in our cluttered minds. If only we were as good at keeping alive our life-giving thoughts as we are at nurturing these weeds! It's moments like these when I recognize the blessing of addiction. Yes, you read that right. The blessing of addiction. The AA way of recovery is to take one day at a time. We don't look to the past with regret, and we don't fear what lies ahead. The only moment in life we are ever guaranteed is the one that we're presently living in.

And yet, as much as I hold to this way of life, I am also no stranger to what I refer to as "unforeseen residual suffering." The "experts" after Sandy Hook warned us that the real trauma and damage wouldn't present itself for ten years. *Ten years!* And lo and behold, the experts were right. Eight years later, and we've already seen a rise in cases of anxiety, depression, and addiction. Suicide and divorce have wreaked havoc on the lives of the hopeless. There's just no way to measure the emotional and psychological damage that results from a tragedy like Sandy Hook, or any significant trauma. And so I have to wonder: After more than a year of social isolation, economic stress, continuous media coverage, and barriers to mental health treatment, where will we be ten years from now? How will this play out? It's a waiting game with no definite answers. And many of us, on the brink of despair, are wondering how in the world we'll muster up the patience to survive one more day.

And yet, all hope isn't lost for those who run to their mother.

## Mary's Heroic Patience

We all lose our patience with things, events, and people … and even with God. What does patience with God look like? It looks like trust and waiting in times of difficulty when nothing goes our way. It looks like remaining obedient to the will of God despite not having the breakthrough, cure, or answer we desire. Our Lady was most obedient to the will of God without having any certainty. She never asked, "How long, Lord?" She never demanded to see more than one step ahead. Mary is our perfect model, offering practical and prayerful ways to handle the fear of uncertainty and temper our need to know what comes next. There are three tips from Mary that I want to focus on particularly.

First, trust God's Word. This young maiden at the Annunciation agrees to an unimaginable invitation, without certainty or details of the future. The ardent desire of Mary's heart to do the will of God trumped the desire for more information and put her fear to rest. We tend to steer where we stare. Looking at information instead of looking at God rarely quiets our hearts, but instead instills greater fear. Remember, it's okay to be afraid; even Mary had to be told to "Be not afraid." It's what we do with that fear that makes all the difference. What did Mary do? She asked how she could cooperate, and then she pondered. In other words, she remained in the present moment with God, believing what Scripture said about her circumstance: "For with God nothing will be impossible" (Lk 1:37).

In addition to fear, Mary also felt anxiety. When Jesus was twelve years old, and the Holy Family was returning home from Jerusalem, he stayed behind without his parents knowing. Mary and Joseph went a day's journey before realizing he wasn't among

the caravan. After three days of their faith and patience being tested, they finally found Jesus in the Temple. "Son, why have you
treated us so? Behold, your father and I have been looking for
you anxiously" (Lk 2:48). Three days! I once lost my five-year-old
daughter at the beach for about ten minutes, and it was the longest,
most frantic ten minutes of my life. I ran up and down the shore
calling out her name, scanning the surface of the ocean, and fear-
ing the worst. Once I found her, happily walking in the opposite
direction from where we were stationed, pink cheeked and freck-
led, searching for shells, I didn't know what I wanted to do more:
to hug her or kill her. But from Mary, we learn another response to
the child who tries our patience. Mary pondered. After Jesus asks,
"Did you not know that I must be in my Father's house?" Mary,
despite not fully understanding, doesn't give way to anger or lose
her patience with her seemingly snarky child. Instead, she "kept
all these things in her heart." Knowing who her Son was, and what
he was called to be, no other response would do. Jesus wasn't being
rude to his mother, but reminding her of his mission. "The story
conveys a truth that runs sharply counter to our sensibilities: even
the most powerful familial emotions must, in the end, give way to
mission." Every day with Jesus was another "yes" to God. Trusting
in God's plan, Mary could patiently ponder as, bit by bit, she let
her Son go.

Mary also understood that God's plan would involve great
suffering. Yet we never read about Mary asking God to hurry up
and end the pain. No Bible verse quotes Mary's impatience in the
process or tearful plea that God pull the sword from her heart and
put an end to her sorrow. That's what we do. I'm presently in year
eight of one trauma-related issue after the next and asking, *Can
we be done with this now, Lord? Six years is good, right? We can end
this at six.* Mary was never interested in rushing through God's
plan. I imagine her pondering revolved around this one question:
*What do you want me to learn from this?*

Second, don't go back to Egypt. In Exodus, when the journey started to feel too long for the Israelites and complaining got the best of them, they looked back to what they'd left behind. And I get it. When there's no end in sight, you forget that God has a plan, and you just want to go back to how things used to be — even if they weren't that good. This is where we need to turn to Mary. From the moment she gave her *fiat*, she faced one obstacle after the next. She had to leave her hometown, give birth in a stable, flee to Egypt ... I mean, seriously! We'd completely understand if Mary had jumped off that donkey and run back home crying to her mother. But she didn't. Trusting in God's Word, she didn't run backward, but remained in place, pondering God's will in that moment. This posture of heart-pondering prayer is where we learn true patience.

Finally, Mary teaches us to keep an upward perspective. Because of her pondering, Mary had her heart set firmly on the goal of life: heaven. While she lived firmly in the present moment with God, she also kept her eyes on the true prize. We forget this when our lives are fraught with fear. If our focus is more on the race than it is on the prize, we'll drop dead from exhaustion. This race requires perseverance, which means we must put on our blinders, turn off the world, and keep looking upward, knowing we were created for heaven.

Are we almost there yet? That isn't for us to know, and we ought not to waste the time the Lord gives us by praying to get past the waiting, or complaining that he's taking too long. The waiting is where our transformation happens. The goal of our lives, contrary to what the world says, isn't to make ourselves as happy and comfortable as possible on earth, but to bear all temporal sorrows patiently, after the example of Christ, so that we can enjoy life in heaven. Following Christ means we imitate Christ. If Christ suffered patiently, then so should we. In *The Imitation of Christ* we read: "My child, I came down from heaven to save you; I took upon Myself your miseries, not because I had to do so, but out of love. I wanted you to learn patience and to bear the trials of this life without complaint, as I have done for you."

We only have to look at the lives of the saints to be reminded of this. Mother Teresa, who was a picture of joy, confessed to having suffered a "dark night of the soul" for eleven years. When nearly at the point of despair, she recognized that her painful longing was actually a share in the thirst of Jesus. She writes, "For the first time in this 11 years — I have come to love the darkness. For I believe now that it is a part, a very, very small part of Jesus' darkness and pain on earth." Mother Teresa had the strength and patience to persevere because she recognized the purpose of long-suffering: It was a mysterious link to the Lord's suffering. It was what united her to the Heart of Jesus.

Our Lady, at the foot of the cross, was the first person to hear Jesus cry, "I thirst." Mary stood and watched her son die of thirst, for us. How long did those torturous hours feel? How long did the three days before his resurrection painfully drag on? How about the three days he was lost, before being found in the Temple? Or every time she changed his diaper, gave him a bath, or held his hand, knowing that her wholehearted embrace of God's will meant that her child would be "set for the fall and rising of many in Israel"? God asked Mary to stand at the foot of the cross because "without Our Lady, we would be … alone before the crosses of life, oblivious to Jesus in our midst." When our suffering is long, and we're on the brink of despair, Mary is with us.

We can have patience because everything life sends our way is an opportunity for spiritual gain. Pandemics, politics, hard relationships, tragedies, addiction — whatever it is God is asking you to wait in, please don't think of it as something you need to get over. Instead, focus on the virtue you need to get under it. Invite the Holy Spirit into the waiting and imitate Mary, who didn't refuse the suffering of her crucified Son, but endured it with heroic patience, knowing that all we suffer for God comes with great merit. There's no question, life is a battle and God will call us to situations that feel impossible and endless. Our faith will be tested, and getting angry at God and turning our backs on him when he makes us wait too long might feel better than sticking it out and trusting that he is up to something good. If this is where you are right now, take your eyes off the clock and put them on Mary. Mary, who never said, "I can't endure this" or "This is too much" or "What you ask of me is impossible." Mary, the ultimate female superhero, waited with God patiently until winning her crown.

Like Mary, it's by holy patience that we make our way to the Lord, who is our goal. Heaven is what we're after. We want the crown. *The Imitation of Christ* urges us: "So be ready to fight to win the victory. Without a conflict, you cannot obtain the crown of patience. If you reject the suffering, you reject the crown also; but if you wish to be crowned, resist strongly and patiently."

In today's world of instant everything, this virtue of heroic patience might be the most difficult to obtain and the one we need most. Perhaps reflecting on these words of Bishop Barron can help: "Waiting is the delay of what we want. But there is much happening in the waiting. We embrace the waiting when we wait with God. There is a difference between waiting for God to do something versus waiting with God as he does something." So let's take Mary's hand and patiently wait with God. With her help, we can trust that he's doing something good.

— 7 —

# Embracing Your Cross with Firm Peace

✟

I was living in a railroad apartment on the upper east side of New York City when I received my first credit card statement in the mail. I don't recall the total owed, but my guess is that I'd purchased a few items at The Gap, and had run up a bill. I was in my early twenties, unmarried, working full time at a talent agency downtown, and making decent money. I also had parents who helped me with rent, no kids, no student loans, no car payments or insurance, and so I'm certain that whatever that bill was for, I had the money to cover it. As I reached for my checkbook, however, something at the top of the bill caught my eye. Two words I had never considered: minimum payment. How wonderful, I thought, that I don't have to pay it all right now! How kind of the credit card company to let me take as long as I wanted to pay this off!

And thus began my disordered attachment to, and dysfunctional relationship with, money.

Ten years later, married with four kids, living in Los Angeles, financial peace was not a thought in our minds. In fact, we had no idea that the words "financial" and "peace" could ever coexist. Always struggling to make ends meet, we justified the use of our credit cards; we had no other choice but to run them up. In our defense, we truly did believe that in a year we would be better off and have the money to cover the bills. But every year would come and go, and usually it'd bring us another baby, and well, have you ever had a baby? Because they're not free.

For the majority of our married life, my husband and I have been living in the opposite of financial peace — whatever you want to call that. Financial chaos, stress, anxiety, resentment, and worry, maybe. Interestingly, according to an article published by Dave Ramsey Solutions, a program built on a Christian foundation that teaches you how to have financial peace, money is the second leading cause of divorce. I think the reason why money isn't the number one reason for divorce is because people with money problems can't afford to get divorced. I'm kind of joking, but also kind of serious. Years ago in a heated argument, my husband blurted out, "Maybe I should just leave!" And I remember thinking, *We only have one car ... probably not wise. And we can barely pay the rent for this house. Where would you even go?* I mean, I suppose he could've lived in the car, but that would've been awkward because again, we only had the one car. Poverty saved our marriage.

A lot of couples fight about money, while others avoid the topic altogether. We developed the habit of avoiding it. My husband was, and still is, a hard worker. I'd picked up a side hustle baking cakes while managing the kids and home. We were doing everything we could to keep our heads above water, and so I could never understand why we were always drowning. Looking back, I realize it was our habit of avoiding the issue that sunk our ship. We had become experts at avoiding the truth: We were in serious financial trouble. How could we let things get so bad?

In my husband's defense, I made it impossible for him to approach me honestly about our situation. I was highly sensitive and terribly afraid, and as soon as he started mentioning our debt, I'd start to cry, which made him get defensive, and then I'd resent him, and good grief, I wouldn't approach myself if I had to!

In my defense, I didn't know any better. I'd developed zero good habits when it came to money, and I assumed that my husband would take care of everything. And so when I failed to offer my husband safety in coming to me, he responded by not offering me the security I needed from him. We charged together into bankruptcy, but I believed it was up to him to protect me from it. And so, as the arguments escalated along with the "total amount due," my husband did the only logical thing he knew to do at the moment. He took all our bills, threw them in a duffel bag, zipped it up, and hid it in the back of our closet.

Ask me how that went.

We all have a duffel bag stashed in the back of our closet, don't we? You may even have more than one. It's what we like to do with the crosses we've been given that we don't want to deal with. My husband and I can look back and laugh at how ridiculous that was, but at the time we were truly afraid. There was so much discord, agitation, and stress, that we knew no other way around it. Perhaps that was because God wasn't calling us to go around it. He was inviting us to walk through it. Our pride prevented us from accepting it, and so we chose to stuff it, zip it, and hide it instead. Contrary to what you might believe, while we were not smart about the way we handled our money, the real reason our lives lacked peace had nothing to do with money. We lacked peace because we lacked humility.

For the longest time, I thought that peace was achieved by eliminating suffering. That as soon as *this* was resolved, or *that* was over, then I'd find peace. But, in fact, that can't be the case because, should we fully eliminate suffering, how many of us would consider Christ ever again? Thomas à Kempis writes: "In this mortal life, our peace consists in the humble bearing of suffering and contradictions, not in being free of them, for we cannot live in this world without adversity. Those who can best suffer will enjoy the most peace, for such persons are masters of themselves, lords of the world, with Christ for their friend and heaven as their reward."

When Saint Paul speaks about joy and peace, he exhorts us to "Rejoice in the Lord always! I shall say it again: rejoice!" He says that it is by "prayer and supplication with thanksgiving" that the "peace of God, which passes all understanding, will keep your hearts and your minds in Christ Jesus" (Phil 4:6–7). He says nothing about needing to be free from trials to obtain this peace. Rather, we must center our lives on Christ while suffering.

Paul understood that suffering is the cross, and the cross *is* life. It's the cross that leads us to the Kingdom. Not Starbucks. Not football; not your promotion; not how well you maintain a clean kitchen; but the cross. That's why we can count on this one thing: There will always be a cross. When God takes one cross from us, he hands us another. And sure, for someone who doesn't know Jesus, this sounds terrible. But for us, this is truly sweet news. "Behold the cross is all and in dying to thyself all consists," writes Thomas à Kempis, "and there is no other way to life and to true internal peace but the holy way of the cross." Peace, my friend, is born of humility, not of perfect circumstances. It's only by persevering in suffering that we obtain inner peace.

I can't even begin to count the number of times I've pushed away the chalice offered to me, thinking that by refusing to drink it, I'd create peace in my life. Just the opposite happened. I needed Mary, the Queen of Peace, to help me achieve true, lasting peace like hers.

## Mary's Firm Peace

Mary drank the chalice to the dregs because she had full confidence and trust in God. She was filled with peace because she was full of God. She's the Queen of Peace because she's the mother of the Prince of Peace.

With Mary, we must seek peace, not as the world gives it, but as Jesus offers: "Peace I leave with you; my peace I give to you; not as the world gives do I give to you. Let not your hearts be troubled, neither let them be afraid" (Jn 14:27). Jesus is clear. We can count on trouble, yet peace is possible because the peace that our hearts long for comes through him. "I have said this to you, that *in me* you may have peace. In the world you *have tribulation*; but be of good cheer, I have overcome the world" (Jn 16:33, emphases added). The peace we yearn for only comes from Jesus. So why do we insist on searching everywhere else?

Because finding real peace first requires that we accept real pain: that we step into the fire, reach for the cup, and drink it to the dregs. Most of us don't want to do that. Our human instinct is to run out of a burning building, not into it. It's the natural human response to keep away from what threatens to burn us. I do this with the crosses I'm sent. Not all of them, but definitely the ones that threaten to consume me like fire. I run from, not toward them.

We all have a cross we try to leave behind and an arena engulfed in flames that the Lord is calling us to stand in the center of. And boy, do we want to run. Yet running away from the pain never brings peace. Running into it does. As we read in 1 Peter 4:12–13: "Beloved, do not be surprised at the fiery ordeal which comes upon you to prove you, as though something strange were happening to you. But rejoice in so far as you share Christ's sufferings, that you may also rejoice and be glad when his glory is revealed."

Take Mary's hand and run to the cross.

Remember how Mary said, "Let it be to me"? It's important

to note that she said "to me," not "let me do it." Her yes to God was a yes in all things, a complete handing over and total abandonment to his will for her life. Did Mary know *exactly* what God was asking of her at that moment? I don't think so ... not exactly. But Mary wasn't oblivious, either. She was attentive, well-versed in Scripture, and always thinking. She took nothing for granted, but brought every word, every action, every moment, to God. I think we forget to do this. When we've been blindsided, we might kick, scream, and cry, but then we immediately start wringing our hands and running in circles trying to formulate a plan — *our plan.*

In his book *Searching for and Maintaining Peace*, Fr. Jacques Philippe writes, "The measure of our interior peace will be that of our abandonment, consequently of our detachment." If we want to imitate Mary and possess a Marian peace, we need to abandon and detach, keeping in mind that our life, while it may look like a train wreck on the outside, can still be very much at peace. Joy and sorrow can coexist. Grief and gratefulness can walk hand in hand. Mary isn't only Our Lady of Sorrows, but also Our Queen of Peace.

In a 2013 homily, Pope Benedict XVI "proposed Mary's serenity as the source of interior peace and as the foundation for world peace." I found this excerpt from his homily especially relevant for us today:

> We may ask ourselves: what is the basis, the origin, the root of peace? How can we experience that peace within ourselves, in spite of problems, darkness, and anxieties? The reply is given to us by the readings of today's liturgy. The biblical texts, especially the one just read from the Gospel of Luke, ask us to contemplate the interior peace of Mary, the Mother of Jesus. During the days in which "she gave birth to her first-born son" (Lk 2:7), many un-

expected things occurred: not only the birth of the Son but, even before, the tiring journey from Nazareth to Bethlehem, not finding a room at the inn, the search for a chance place to stay for the night; then the song of the angels and the unexpected visit of the shepherds. In all this, however, Mary remains even-tempered, she does not get agitated, she is not overcome by events greater than herself; in silence she considers what happens, keeping it in her mind and heart, and pondering it calmly and serenely. This is the interior peace which we ought to have amid the sometimes tumultuous and confusing events of history, events whose meaning we often do not grasp and which disconcert us.

What robs us of our peace? I believe if we trace back to where the trouble begins, we'll find it lies in our hearts. Mary's pure heart was the driving force behind her peace. Because she lived in a posture of prayer, she was always looking to God, not to herself. Can we say the same about our hearts? When my heart is troubled, it's usually wrestling with a temptation to anger or resentment. Sometimes my peace is stolen from me because I've allowed others' opinions of me to rule my day. Other times, it's despair over a situation where I'm helpless that steals my stillness. When we come to know the human Mary, we recognize that her perfection doesn't mean she was exempt from the things we suffer. Mary felt everything we feel, and even more so, and still she maintained firm inner peace.

Observe how Mary responded to those things that tend to disturb us: She pondered before she reacted. She remembered who God is and the depths of his faithfulness, love, and mercy. She recalled all the ways he'd shown up for her in the past and praised him for being with her in each moment, whether she felt him or not, for she knew that God isn't our feelings, and he's always with us. And she always had before her the fruit of a cross well carried.

If we want true peace to reign in this world, it'll have to flow from us first. We must bear our own crosses peacefully, careful not to become a cross to others. We need to have confidence in God and ponder his ways always, maintaining Mary's firm peace, no matter our circumstances.

— 8 —

# Embracing Your Cross with Profound Humility

✝

Here's the truth: We don't want help. We want to be able to handle everything on our own. Help is for babies, wimps, and failures.

Have you ever felt this way? When did self-reliance become such an important badge of honor? Why do we perceive receiving outside help as a sign of weakness and a set of extra hands pointing to our hands not being enough? Is it just me, or would we rather die doing everything by our strength than let the world in on our deepest secret: We need help.

For many years, the thought of reaching out for help with anything, be it a ride to school for my kids or a call to a therapist for myself, was cause for shame. Needing someone to step in and help carry the cross I believed Jesus gave to me to carry alone made me feel like a failure. A perfectionist to the core, I thought being perfect meant carrying the weight of the world on my own, while maintaining a clean house and a thin body, with a line of well-behaved kids in tow.

By the time I gave birth to our second-born, we were living in Los Angeles, two thousand miles away from friends and family. We'd been warned not to move far from free babysitting, but we didn't listen because we had a plan. My husband, an actor by day, hotel doorman by night, had a buddy out West offering him a "real job" with his internet company. We weren't going to stay there forever, maybe a year — just long enough to make a ton of money. That was our drive and our motive: money. Unfortunately, the job fell through, my husband had to fall back on his acting, and I remained perpetually pregnant, turning one year in L.A. into ten years stuck in L.A. We had a small handful of friends and a spirited two-year-old when we welcomed our new baby girl. Nick was back to working late-night shifts as a doorman, because that is what "falling back on your acting career" looks like, while I tried to manage a toddler and newborn in a new city, all on my own. It was a challenge, for sure, but I was determined to do it.

A week after Belle was born, we were blessed with a visit by my mom. She was going to stay for a week to help us adjust and offer a pair of extra hands. The woman is amazing. You can have absolutely nothing in the fridge (and I mean nothing), and she will make a ten-course meal out of it. She's the original Chopped Kitchen. I swear! All that we had in the cupboards was a brick and a tomato, and somehow she made a chicken casserole and tossed salad. She also irons better than any dry cleaner in town, has an insanely green thumb, and she'll make your laundry smell like heaven. Having her around for the week to help out and care for me was such a gift, but it worried me, too. I was afraid of help. What if her help proved that I couldn't manage my family on my own? What if when she left, I started to drown? What if she saw how incapable I was of running a household? And how the heck do I make dinner out of a brick and tomato? With family so far away, and not being able to afford help moving forward, I never wanted to know what it was like to have the help. And I'd rather have drowned in secret than ask a friend for help.

We're so afraid of people seeing how we really live, aren't we?

God never intended for us to handle it all. He asks us to hand it all over. Jesus himself left us an example to imitate by accepting help from Simon of Cyrene, whom they "compelled to carry his cross" (Mt 27:32). If God himself had help carrying his cross, what makes me believe that I should carry mine alone? God never intends for us to carry our crosses alone. This was a lesson I had to learn the hard way, years after my mother's helpful visit.

It was Advent 2012 when our Sandy Hook community was shaken. A decorated Christmas tree stood tall in the corner of the living room. We'd gone out as a family to chop it down at the tree farm just a few days before the shooting. We were looking forward to taking in all the holiday festivities and buying and wrapping gifts. After December 14, the calendar days leading up to Christmas day were filled with a different kind of running around — planned community activities to distract our children and funerals for the all-too-aware adults to attend. In the midst of this, I came down with the flu. Winter in all her darkness, barrenness, and chill lived up to her name. I was helpless to do anything, mentally and physically wrecked.

They say that in the wake of tragedy or misfortune you find out who your true friends are. John 15:13 tells us, "Greater love has no one than this, that a man lay down his life for his friends." And Proverbs 17:17 stipulates that "a friend loves at all times." It took this dark season for us to recognize such friends. I remember getting the phone call from my friend Jane, back in Los Angeles.

"Give us your list," she lovingly insisted.

"My what?"

"Your list ... the kids' Christmas list. Your west coast elves are going to shop for you."

These friends weren't just going to do the shopping, but the wrapping as well. They wanted to be certain that Nick and I didn't have to worry about anything other than sliding the gifts underneath the tree. This was beautiful, true friendship ... and difficult to accept on so many levels. I hated that I needed help. I like to do things on my own, and I don't like people seeing my mess. If you peered into my kitchen cabinets (or, God forbid, the linen closet), you might never look at me the same way again. You also might need a rabies shot. But this time was different, because I had no choice. The cross was bigger than any other cross I'd attempted to carry alone. I was forced to set pride aside and embrace the one virtue that I'd avoided so well my entire life: *humility.*

Have you ever prayed the Litany of Humility? If not, go ahead, I dare you. And if you have, terrifying, isn't it? I mean, this prayer gets right down to it. Yet it's a prayer that we all need, especially when it comes to allowing people to help us carry our crosses. Mankind has struggled with pride from the beginning, when Adam and Eve fell into sin because they wanted to be like God. Every time we fall into self-reliance and self-centeredness, we eliminate God from the equation. We deny any help that doesn't come from within, and we pick up our cross, putting faith in ourselves. We believe the lie that we've got everything under control. And then we fall beneath the weight of our cross.

The great surprise of that Advent cross was learning to let go and let God. By allowing my friends to step in and help, I allowed Jesus to step in and work through them. It was his eyes that looked at shelves and chose toys and dolls. It was his hands that wrapped each gift. It was his heart that bled for our wounded community. And the way that he loved us that Christmas was through the hands and hearts of people who didn't merely ask if they could help, but insisted on it. The grace of the virtue of humility was the best gift I could've received that year. It not only taught me that the way to carry the cross with faith is by carrying it with others, but that when you invite people to participate in your suffering, the fruits that flow from the cross are beyond anything you could ever imagine.

Nothing teaches us the virtues better than the cross, and no one models this for us better than Mary.

## Mary's Profound Humility

"Perfect humility," writes Fr. Raniero Cantalamessa, "consists in constantly making oneself small, not for the sake of some personal need or benefit, but for the sake of love, to elevate others." This is the humility of Our Lady, the humility that God is so attracted to. Fr. Peter Cameron writes, "More than anything else, what moved God to act [at the Annunciation] was the humility He found in the Blessed Virgin." This is why we need and should fight for this virtue. Without humility, we're unable to fully open ourselves up to the grace that can only come from God, the grace we need to become the people God created us to be. Mary, the lowly servant and handmaid of the Lord, embraces this virtue fully, not for her benefit, but for ours. And after she gives her amazing *fiat*, she runs in haste to visit her cousin, for the sake of love.

The Visitation is the immediate movement of Mary following the Son of God's conception in her womb. This visitation is no ordinary road trip to hang with an old friend. Mary's on a mission. Saint Bonaventure says, "The Creator of all things rests in the tabernacle of the virginal womb," and so Mary runs in haste to bring the Presence of God to another. And not just *any* other, but her cousin Elizabeth, who after years of being barren, is now also with child "through a mystery of mercy." What an incredible moment between friends! And what draws me in further is the humility on both parts. The humility of Mary, who in her Magnificat announces, "for he who is mighty has done great things for me, and holy is his name." And the humility of Elizabeth, who cries, "And why is this granted me, that the mother of my Lord should come to me?"

I've often thought about Mary as she "went with haste into the hill country, to a city of Judah" (Lk 1:39). She was a young, pregnant woman. How did she get there alone? How long was the trip? Did she pack snacks? Where did she sleep? How did she know the directions without the help of a GPS? Seriously, these are the things that I wondered about until reading Fr. Donald Calloway's book, *Consecration to St. Joseph: The Wonders of Our Spiritual Father*. Calloway presents another perspective on the Visitation: that Mary didn't go alone to her cousin's house. Joseph accompanied her. Could it be that Mary had help on the journey?

Calloway writes:

> Many saints and mystics — St. Bernard of Clairvaux, St. Bonaventure, St. Bernardine of Siena, St. Francis de Sales, Venerable Mary of Agreda, Blessed Anne Catherine Emmerich, and others — believe that St. Joseph did accompany Mary to Elizabeth's. Why wouldn't he go with her? What kind of husband would he be if he let his young and beautiful wife make such a long journey unaccompanied by her husband?

The sacred text doesn't tell us that Mary asked for Joseph's help, but it doesn't tell us that she didn't, either. Nor is it clear that Joseph insisted on escorting her. All that we know is that Mary went in haste. The more I entertain Father Calloway's theory, the more sense it makes. What man would let his beloved wife go on such a journey alone? And what woman would refuse the protection of such a holy and just man? I like to believe that, in her humility, Mary welcomed the help of her spouse; that she didn't look at him cross-eyed and snap, "What? You think I need a man? You think I can't take care of myself? In case you haven't heard, the future is female, Joe, get on board!" On the contrary, what made this holy couple so holy was their appreciation for God's creation of man and woman, the specific attributes he gave to each, and the way they complement one another. I think Mary, in all her humility and self-knowledge, would've humbly asked for Joseph's help; and in his righteousness, he would've been more than happy to do what he knew God had called him to do: protect the Mother and Son of God.

Mary not only relied on Joseph's help, but Elizabeth's as well! Nothing consoles us more than two simple words: Me, too. I just love how the angel made sure to mention Elizabeth's miracle pregnancy to Mary before leaving her alone to ponder. "And behold, your kinswoman Elizabeth in her old age has also conceived a son; and this is the sixth month with her who was called barren" (Lk 1:36). In other words, "You're not alone. Someone else understands." No wonder Mary went in haste! Imagine the loneliness she would've felt, isolated in her home, unable to explain her situation — one which could have been cause for her being stoned to death — because no one could possibly understand. No one but Elizabeth, that is. How good is our God to give us these kinds of friends? Friends that we can share the unbelievable with, and they can believe, because they, too, have been through something similar. Mary may have been all sold out for God with an unwavering "yes" to his will on her lips, but she was also a human in need of consolation. And she wasn't afraid to seek it out.

Mary could've stayed home with Jesus in her womb. In times of uncertainty, when we face the possibility of great humiliation, isn't that our safest bet? When conspiracy theorists were banging on my front door, and I couldn't walk two steps outside without the fear of being followed, attacked, or someone shoving the news in my face, the only place I ran in haste to was my bed. Mary shows us another way to respond to our crosses. Why do I call this a cross? Because, while the birth of Jesus was a miracle, a great gift, and a cause for joy, let's not forget where Mary's "yes" takes her: It leads her to the foot of the cross. In fact, her "yes" guaranteed the cross. Yet Mary picks herself up and sets out on her journey, and I have to believe that God wants the same for us. When we, too, are filled with Jesus, we must run in haste to bring him to others, especially those who are suffering. And when we're the ones in pain, we can hope that someone out there will run in haste to us, bringing the presence of Jesus to us.

Suffering is difficult. But suffering alone is unbearable. To get past the suffering, we need to swim through the pain to others. We need to accept it, feel it, and when it hurts too much, swim all the harder until we at last rise above it. Because we will. Jesus will even throw us a life vest, in the form of other people, so we can catch our breath and be renewed and rested to begin swimming again. Remember, too, that the cross doesn't last forever. Jesus hung on the cross for three hours, not forever, and he wasn't alone. Simon helped him carry his cross, and Veronica courageously stepped out of the crowd and wiped his face clean. What consolation these encounters must have been to Mary, as she knew that she couldn't prevent what was happening. And as her Son hung on the cross, we find the beloved apostle John standing by Mary's side. She didn't push him away, or resist his comfort, but welcomed his loving embrace. If Jesus invited people to participate in his passion, accepting help along the way, why on earth do we think we have to figure out our cross on our own? Why do we think we can carry our cross better than Jesus? Why do we insist on standing alone, when the Mother of God did not?

It comes down to humility. Unless we empty ourselves of self and make room for the Holy Spirit to take up residence in our soul, we'll forever follow those who preach a false gospel. The influencers shout, "Don't accept less than you deserve!" or "Don't make yourself small!" or "It's your life, and you are in control!" The message is untrue and unbiblical. Our story never begins with us, but with a baby — a king, our Creator and God of the universe — born to a lowly handmaid in a stable. A dirty, stinky stable that was all that her spouse could provide — something tells me that this wasn't something she made Joseph feel badly about, but accepted gratefully. God chose flesh, a mother, and poverty. God, though infinite and the all-powerful source of all life, chose to become human. Though he was sinless, he chose to die on a cross for our sins. God chose the very last place in the world so that he could have the very first place in our hearts. And Mary, without boasting, bragging, or making a big deal of it, simply agreed to it all, keeping much of it hidden, yet proclaiming the greatness of God from the depths of her soul.

In the world's eyes, shouldn't the Mother of God give birth in the greatest of conditions? That woman's hospital bedding should've been a 350-thread count, at the minimum! The Mother of God should be regarded as the greatest among us, the topic of all our discussions, the account with the most hits and followers. Instead, Mary stepped into her incredible role with zero notice and total abandonment. Her humility is that profound.

How do you feel about making yourself lowly? Is that something you pray for? Maybe you slip that intention somewhere in between *Please help me land that promotion at work that I fear will go to Bob, who by the way, doesn't deserve it* and *Help me with my golf swing so that I can win today's game.* Lowliness is usually not at the top of our list. If it were, I wonder if our crosses would be lighter. Lack of humility in a dark season adds weight to the cross. Why? Because if we had humility as profound as Mary's, we'd have no problem asking for help. We'd go in haste and share what's happening inside of us. We'd rejoice in our need for others. We'd recognize that when we allow others to enter into our suffering, something very sacred and holy happens. We discover what it means to be the Body of Christ. We discover what it means to be united in Christ by its members. We finally understand what our mothers meant by telling us to "offer it up." We discover the fruits of our cross.

Years ago, I received a most interesting response to an article I'd published on suffering from a woman who frequented my writing space and had no belief in God. Regarding the cross, she wrote, "I do not see how you can look at that and see love." I found it almost impossible to respond because I don't know how to look at the cross and see anything *but* Love. It's only at the foot of the cross that I feel safe enough to curl up like a child and let it all out. The cross beckons me to lower myself, unclench my hands, and face my spiritual poverty. Everywhere else in this world I feel the pull toward pride, grasping at things, and needing to prove myself. This is a huge problem, especially when you consider that "the first condition for receiving the benefits of the Kingdom," as Joseph Langford reminds us, "is that of receiving it as a child, humbly yet joyfully recognizing and accepting our need for the living waters." Moreover, "Those who attempt to enter the Kingdom through their own self-sufficiency or self-made holiness will be, in the words of Our Lady, 'cast down from their thrones' and 'sent away empty.'"

Pride keeps us in a posture of resistance before the cross. Humility puts us in a posture of acceptance. When we can name our suffering and tell the Lord about it and ask for his help, we break down barriers. Then beautiful and unexpected things flow, not from us, but from the cross — things like empathy, caring, compassion, and selflessness. When we bring others into our story of suffering and allow them to share in the heavy lifting, we create a new space for God. We dig a well of self-knowledge that helps us to recognize not only our poverty and thirst for love, but this same deep thirst in others. We are no longer inclined to stare at ourselves, marinating in the pity of our present sorrow, boasting of our self-reliance; instead, we prefer to look up and out, to step out of our story and enter into another's. We can learn to rejoice in the good things that happen to others, because we no longer see ourselves as separate temples, but knit together, forming the Church. It's only when we accept our littleness, when we approach the throne of God as a small child, that we can bear to come face to face with our worthlessness. And when we do this, when we get small enough to admit that we need the help of others — oh, the fruit of the cross!

As I encourage you to bring others into your story, to allow trusted friends — life vests from Jesus — to step into your suffering, wrap you with hope, and help you swim up, let me offer you this piece of advice: Start with Mary.

The first step to carrying your cross with faith is to invite Mary into your home, as Joseph did after the Annunciation (see Mt 1:24). If you ask for her heart, she'll lend it to you; she'll teach you how to walk the road of the cross with humility and grace if you depend on her. St. Louis de Montfort assures us, "We make more progress in a brief period of submission to and dependence on Mary than in whole years of following our own will and relying upon ourselves." With the virtue of profound humility, we can stand before the cross with an open heart and hands. We can accept help when it's offered, no longer ashamed of our weakness, but grateful for it, because we walk the path of Mary.

Of this path, de Montfort states:

> We do find, it is true, great battles to fight, and great hardships to master; but that good Mother makes herself so present and so near to her faithful servants, to enlighten them in their darkness and their doubts, to strengthen them in their fears, and to sustain them in their struggles and difficulties, that in truth this virginal path to find Jesus Christ is a path of roses and honey compared with the

other paths.

I don't pretend that humility is easy, but with the help of Mary's example, I've tasted its sweetness. It's the sweetness of a path that never demands we carry our cross on our own, but beckons us to bring in our neighbor. Mary's path reminds us that the degree of our lowliness on earth will be the degree of our greatness in glory.

# — 9 —

# Embracing Your Cross with Angelic Sweetness

✝

I once told a priest in confession that I'm "bitey." Don't bother to look that up in the dictionary, it's not a real word. But it's exactly how it sounds. The bitey one is inclined to, well … bite. It usually happens in a conversation that stirs up a cocktail of unhealthy emotions and untrue thoughts. I feel like I've been wronged and need to defend myself. And so, I bite. I know when it's happening, and I want more than anything to hold back, fight the temptation, and offer up all the raging fury in my heart for the souls in purgatory, but I rarely do. Sorry, souls. The struggle on earth is real. My words lunge with no fair warning. They're aggressive. They pierce. They hurt. And I always walk away hating myself, because biting other people doesn't feel good. I know that bites can leave lasting marks — wounds and scars. If I were a dog, I would've been put down years ago.

The priest in that confessional leaned in and said, "Wouldn't it be great if we could freeze-frame time?" I had to agree. I'd regret so much less if such a thing were possible!

But I'm the bitey one. The loud one. The bold one. The sarcastic one. The quick-witted one. The funny one. The rowdy one. For years, there's been a tug-of-war in my heart between who I am and the sweet person I long to be. I realized I can't do what the Lord is asking me to do — speaking and preaching and encouraging crowds of people, publishing my life, and swimming against the tide — if I never bite. In fact, without a bit of biteyness, I might be eaten alive. I need to be able to bite sometimes, being in the business of *Here's my life, now comment away and don't hold back!* But the question is, can I be bitey and sweet?

I understand that trials and suffering and people who say stupid things to me are a part of this life. And not just a part of it, but a necessary pathway to heaven. They're the obstacles that become opportunities to make me holy. I really do understand this. But in the heat of the moment, I make an impulsive move, and good luck trying to get me to stop. It's like I don't know anything about Jesus, and all I want is to make it very clear that I'm unhappy. My entire being is drained of sweetness. Padre Pio said, "Let us remember that the lot of chosen souls is to suffer." In response I ask, "Can I choose another lot?"

I know that my lot isn't given in vain, nor as punishment for past sins. We often see tragedies and misfortunes and all the painful occurrences in our lives as God's way of saying, "Remember that argument with your spouse and that unkind thing you said? Well, this is for that!" Instead, as St. Padre Pio said, the suffering and trials that are unique to our lives have been chosen for us. Our particular cross is our pathway to heaven. But Padre Pio also said something else that helps us to understand this "chosen lot" a much better. He said that we ought to "let all our concern be to love God and be pleasing to Him" and "God, the Author of all grace and of every gift leading to salvation, has decreed that glory will be ours on condition that we endure suffering with a Christian spirit."

Awareness of sin and the desire to change is the beginning of our transformation. And trust me, the enemy would love nothing more than for me to remain unaware and go on biting everything and everyone in sight. Or, even better, to be aware but too prideful to do anything about it, and so fall into a pit of despair and shame. Because the irony of my biting is that it leads to the biting of my own you-know-what. And so, I've resolved to do better. I refuse to lose any more territory than I already have. I stand my ground. I've already spent time with my old friend, despair, in that pit, and it's, well, the pits. Only by God's grace was I able to climb my way out, and I'm confident that it was Our Lady whose sweet hand never let go of mine, who guided that final hoist up and over, out of the pit and into the arms of Jesus. Mary doesn't bite. Is there anyone sweeter than Mother Mary?

I want Mary's virtue of angelic sweetness. Just like that obnoxious girl in *Willy Wonka and the Chocolate Factory* who eyed the golden goose egg and whined, "I want it now." How do we grow in the virtue of angelic sweetness? Well, it's not by being obnoxious and demanding, that much I know. Actually, I know more than that. I happen to have stumbled upon the secret to obtaining this virtue. It's suffering with a Christian spirit. That's it! Were you hoping for something that didn't involve suffering? Sorry. Kind of what this entire book is about.

## Mary's Angelic Sweetness

One year at Christmas time, I was en route to Pennsylvania to give a talk on Advent and decided to make a quick trip to the DMV, just for fun. Kidding, of course. The DMV is neither quick nor fun. My daughter was joining me on the trip, and her learner's permit test was scheduled that same morning. I'd been gifted, just days earlier, with a beautiful miraculous medal. Certain that I'd need Mama Mary's help for my talk, I put that medal on as if I were dressing for battle. When we sat down in the DMV, I noticed that the medal was gone. The beaded chain was still around my neck, but Mary was mysteriously missing. I looked everywhere — on my person, under the seat, on the floor, back to the car, under the car seats, combing the path that I'd walked from the car to the DMV. Nothing. I proceeded to ask the woman at the desk, the guard, and the man at the coffee kiosk. No one had seen my medal. People around me started to ask what I was searching for. "Mary," I said. "I lost a medal of Our Blessed Mother." I couldn't believe it. How was this even possible? Where did she go? Hoping she'd appear in the car after we arrived in Pennsylvania and unloaded our suitcases, I searched that van high and low. Still, no sign of Mary. I'd have to give my talk without her.

Ten months later, in a fit of frustration after my last pair of glasses broke, I found myself searching in the back pocket of my purse for the tiny screw that holds them together. Of course, not being able to see without glasses, this proved difficult. As my hand swept the inside pocket, what felt like a coin touched the tips of my fingers. It was my miraculous medal! She must've silently slipped from my neck, flown down my shirt, and into the pocket of my purse. As I sat there staring in amazement at her, I wondered: How often do I search everywhere for Jesus, except where he is? How many times do I believe he's far from me, when he couldn't be any closer? I might've lost sight of Mary, but she never lost sight of me. She was with me. Like an angel, she flew to me. And if Mary's with me, then guess who else is with me? Jesus. Because that's what Mary does. She brings us to Jesus and Jesus to us. How does she do this? Angelically! Sweetly!

Mary's angelic sweetness led her always to give way to the impulse to bring others into the mystery, to draw us toward God. Mary's sweetness permeated her life during times of uncertainty, sorrow, and loss, for her life was a series of silent sufferings strung together by the hand of God. Think about that. The Annunciation: Her fearless "yes" to God meant "no" to herself. The Nativity: The welcome of unexpected visitors who brought gifts that pointed to her new baby's death. The Presentation: She learned that a sword would pierce her heart, and instead of reacting, she pondered. Finding Jesus in the Temple: She lost her Son for three days, and upon finding him, recognized that he was all about the work his Father had for him, and so she must let him go. And then there was the wedding feast at Cana. The event of all events. The moment when the hosts ran out of wine, and so Mary brought their need to Jesus. This was more than Mary being a good Jewish mother. This was Mary doing the will of God, because she knew that, as soon as her son performed this public miracle, God's plan of salvation would be in full effect and there'd be no turning back. And yet, through every situation, Mary remained in an angelic state of sweetness. Her suffering didn't make her bitter. Her sorrow didn't lead to anger. She accepted it all from God, took it all in, and pondered it. Since her only desire for her life was to do the will of God, she could be caring, compassionate and encouraging, no matter the cost.

I wish I could say the same for myself. God is usually the first person I blame for my sorrow. Jesus gets an earful from me when I feel like he hasn't given me what I deserve. This is when my biteyness really strikes. Trust me, if I were presenting my son at the Temple, and some old man holding my baby told me that my kid was going to have a really hard life, and guess what, mine was going to suck too? I'd bite the man's entire head off.

Yet if we really understood what Jesus did on the cross for us, and what it means for our salvation, loving God and pleasing him no matter our lot would be a no-brainer. If only we would close our mouths and open our hands to receive this gift of grace! The end to biteyness and the beginning of sweetness is possible for each of us, but it requires that we invite the Holy Spirit to the party. Pay attention to this, because this is how we carry our cross with a Christian spirit. This is how we say yes to all the crazy crosses God tosses our way. This is how we smile while suffering. We beg the Holy Spirit to consume and possess us, because it's impossible to be filled with the Spirit and bite someone's head off at the same time.

Mary, overshadowed by and espoused to the Spirit, has one concern: to love and please God. Mary wants to open the way for this same Spirit in each of our souls. The Holy Spirit is capable of working miracles beyond our wildest thoughts and imaginations. And the Holy Spirit chose to work in partnership with Mary to bring about these marvels of grace. How beautiful is this Holy Spirit, when we allow him to root everything out of us that's not of Christ, and to fill us up with only what pleases him! This is how we become sweet like Mary.

On February 11, 1858, the Blessed Virgin Mary appeared to Bernadette Soubirous, a fourteen-year-old girl at the grotto of Massabielle near the village of Lourdes in France. Bernadette didn't know who the woman was, but she described her as "the beautiful lady." No doubt, Mary was physically beautiful, but what makes her the most beautiful lady is her virtue. Just like love, we've gotten beauty wrong. The amount of time we spend focused on fine lines and wrinkles, sagging skin, balding heads, flabby arms, and a gut designed by the NFL should never outweigh the time spent on our interior selves. Inward beauty is what we should all be after. What good is a perfect body if hatred and negativity flow from our heart? What use are toned muscles, a full head of hair, and flawless skin if we're painful to be around? Sweetness flowed from Mary, no matter her circumstance. Whether she was on her knees in the dirt by the manger, or standing strong at the foot of the cross, the path

Mary walked was one of angelic sweetness, and she desires to walk with us on that same path. She takes our hand and guides us to the cross, teaching us to see its beauty and its sweetness.

I've read that it's "only by entering into the sufferings of Christ that we can enter into the sufferings of others." In other words, my pain becomes the well from which I draw out sweetness. This is compassion at its fullest, and without suffering, we can't offer authentic compassion. Without suffering, there would be no impulse to reach out, help others, or lend a hand or listening ear. It's my personal hurt, loss, disappointment, tragedy, and trauma that compel me to connect with others. Nothing heals my own wounds better than tending to the similar wounds of another. I love what American entrepreneur and peak performance expert Ed Mylett says, "If you feel helpless, be helpful." If God chooses to never answer my prayers in the way I think they need to be answered, my knees will continue to hit the ground and my hands will rise high in praise, and on my lips will forever be a song of gratitude. If the only lesson this bitey woman learns from her cross is the way of sweet compassion, that will be more than enough.

My sweetest friend (who prefers to remain hidden) called me to share an experience she had that took her by great surprise. She was getting herself a coffee at the local coffee shop, when on her way out she spotted a gentleman in the corner, sitting alone. She recognized him as a man who'd been in recent public news — a story of unspeakable tragedy, scrutiny, and judgment. As she left the shop, she described what happened next. "Laura," she said in a hushed voice, "I don't know what happened, but the next thing I knew I was being pulled back into the shop, and I sat down across from this man who didn't know me, and I just listened to him share his story ... and cry. A grown man, sobbing in a coffee shop to a total stranger. It broke my heart. I told him I was praying for him. And I will. Every day. I will pray." It's no coincidence that this day happened to be the day that my friend consecrated herself to

Jesus through Mary. It was the Memorial of Our Lady of Sorrows. And I'd bet every dollar I have and everything I own that it was the Holy Spirit that took my friend's arm and led her back into that coffee shop. I'd also bet that Our Lady was sitting with them the entire time. Why? Because usually my friend, as sweet as she is, would rather die than speak up. And yet, there was a fierceness and boldness about her that day.

We don't usually associate fierceness with sweetness, yet I think that's what Mary's angelic sweetness looks like. We tend to conjure up all sorts of fluffy images when we think of angels, but the truth about angels is that they're fierce, often terrifying beings. Their greeting when they appear in Scripture is "Be not afraid." They're anything but cute and cuddly! Mary, like an angel, was a fierce protector of God's eternal plan. When you're a mother who's been invited to participate in the suffering of Our Lord, you need to be fierce and strong. Sweetness isn't the absence of strength, but what infuses it and makes it holy. Maybe my biteyness — at times — is just that. Maybe Mary's angelic sweetness is a virtue offered to people like me. And just as she slipped into my purse pocket unseen, she sits by me now, softening my edges as I write.

Your past, present, and future suffering may never make any sense at all. With years now between myself and tragedy, I still shake my head at what I've had to endure as a mother, because to this day, I can't make sense of it. What I do understand is that I'll never understand, except for this small piece I can comprehend: Jesus carried my sins and suffered and died for me and my eternal salvation, sparing me an eternity in hell. And because my eternal life is certain to last far longer than my earthly life, this is enough. How did I get to this place of surrender? The only possible answer is Mary. She shows me how it's done. She points me in the right direction, modeling the way to live. She's proof that we can carry our cross and still be joyful; that we can endure long periods of suffering and still respond to others with kindness; that we can be sweet and strong; best of all, we can carry our cross while helping someone else carry theirs. This might be the point where our suffering makes the most sense ever. No longer helpless, we become helpful. No longer bitey, we become beautiful. Rage and resentment give way to angelic sweetness — and this, my friend, changes everything.

— 10 —

# Embracing Your Cross with Divine Purity

✝

I used to hear "purity" and immediately think about sexuality and chastity. And while this is a large part of it, Mary has taught me that there's so much more to purity than that. Mary's divine purity means that she has a pure heart that is sold out for God and God alone. It means every action and thought of hers is accompanied by God. Nothing else competes with him, for her heart is detached from everything except God.

We sinners, on the other hand, live with divided hearts — and a divided heart isn't pure. The roots of impurity in my own heart are fertilized by my anger, envy, pride, self-reliance, and greed. These sprouts grow fast and flourish, pushing God out of his rightful place, creating disorder and chaos, taking center stage. One root that I recently uncovered caused me to pause and fall to my knees: the root of feeling like I'm not enough. Granted, it's OK to feel like we're not enough when it reminds us of who is enough. But when "not enough" leads to despair, that's a good indication that we're still holding on to our ungodly self-reliance. When we feel like we're not enough — not enough of a mother, father, spouse, friend, professional, or even disciple — it's because our hearts don't trust that God is enough. Our hearts are divided.

Nothing tests the purity of your heart like being the parent of a teenager during the Coronavirus Pandemic. With schools closed, sports canceled, and the blindside breakup from hell, my daughter began to buckle beneath the weight of one disappointment after the next. I'd love to tell you exactly how she felt, but she wouldn't tell me. She didn't want to talk about it, and this was cause for concern, because we used to talk about everything. My husband, already struggling in that awkward phase of life that is being the father of a teenage girl, was truly at a loss for words and had no idea how to reach out and console her without the fear of her biting his hand off. She walked around the house, a shell of the girl I remembered, pushing me away while she attempted to carry her cross on her own. It took everything in me to resist the temptation to swoop in and swaddle her, read her *Goodnight Moon*, and sing a soft lullaby as I nursed her to sleep. (Did I mention she was seventeen years old?)

I was sharing with a friend how hard this season was. "No matter what Nick and I do or say, what we have done or what we offer, it's like …" Before I could finish my sentence, my friend finished it for me: "You are not enough." And we both stood still for a moment as the words "not enough" flashed like a neon sign above our heads. I went home and pondered this. If I, the woman who gave birth to and protected this child for seventeen years, and my husband, the man who bought her a Cinderella dress and took her on daddy-daughter dates to Disney, were not enough for her, then who was?

When I can't shake a word from my head, it usually means God has written it on my heart, so I immediately went to my friend Merriam-Webster and looked up its meaning. "Enough" is defined as "in or to a degree or quantity that satisfies or that is sufficient or necessary for satisfaction." The words "satisfy" and "sufficient" jumped out at me because, thanks to studying Scripture, I recognize that those words are characteristics of God — not me. Only God satisfies. Only God is sufficient. Therefore, only God is enough.

I was reminded of Saint Paul's words in Philippians 4:12–13: "I know how to be abased, and I know how to abound; in any and all circumstances I have learned the secret of facing plenty and hunger, abundance and want. I can do all things in him who strengthens me." Paul's secret to contentment had nothing to do with what he could give, and everything to do with the actual Giver. Why? Because on his own, he knew he wasn't enough. It was God in him that gave him the power and strength to persevere in every situation. God was his everything. God occupied every nook and cranny of his heart. When Paul realized he wasn't enough, he didn't run to the mall or reach for another beer or spend hours playing backgammon on his phone. He didn't try to numb or distract himself from the uncomfortableness that life so often is. He trusted instead that God would fully supply him with everything he needed. As a result, he could say "yes" to whatever was asked of him, and he could endure tremendous suffering — and good grief, did that guy suffer — because his heart was pure. Everything Paul did was for the glory of God.

Divine purity sounds like a tall order, especially in today's world where sin doesn't matter, and everything is relative, and we can do whatever we want so long as it doesn't hurt anyone. But "impossible" will never be an excuse for a believer, because with God all things are possible. Like Paul, we can learn to live with our hearts focused always on God. And we do this by imitating Mary's virtue of divine purity.

## Mary's Divine Purity

Mary's purity imitates God's purity. That's why St. Louis de Montfort calls her purity "divine," because it's inspired by God and ultimately leads her to him. Mary's purity was her total and complete self-giving to God of body, mind, and soul. Mary was always thinking about God. There was nothing in her heart that competed with him. Free from the disordered desires that you and I have, Mary's response to the angel Gabriel flowed out of this divine purity. It's been said that, based on Mary's response to Gabriel, "she must have resolved to follow a divine calling to consecrated virginity, as a complete self-donation to God." This is why she asks, "How can this be?" Not because she thinks that God is off his rocker, but because she wants to understand how to do his will without turning her back on her vocation.

"Only a heart as pure and detached as Our Lady's could be so completely receptive to the angel's message." This was true at the Annunciation and throughout her life, for Mary had one focus: loving God and doing his will. Well versed in the Scriptures, this young handmaid understood that her "yes" to God was a "yes" she was going to have to give him daily — a "yes" that would steer and guide her every thought and action, as if her very heartbeat was a whispering "yes". Mary understood her role in salvation history just enough to know that the baby she agreed to carry, nurture, and love was going to be sacrificed for the sins of the world. Only a heart of pure love could make such an agreement.

I think about this every morning when I re-consecrate myself to Our Lady with the words of St. Louis de Montfort in his prayer of consecration:

> In the presence of all the heavenly court I choose thee this
> day for my Mother and Mistress. I deliver and consecrate

to thee, as thy slave, my body and soul, my goods, both interior and exterior, and even the value of all my good actions, past, present and future: leaving to thee the entire and full right of disposing of me, and all that belongs to me, without exception, according to thy good pleasure, for the greater glory of God, in time and in eternity.

This is precisely what Our Lady's "yes" embodied. She left to God the entire and full right of disposing of herself, and all that belonged to her, without exception, according to his good pleasure, for God's greater glory.

That "without exception" hit me particularly hard one morning as I was praying for the grace of divine purity. I am to give God everything, without exception: my marriage, children, work, beloved relationships, everything. This isn't easy to do when you hold a degree in Controlling Everything. But do you want to know what I find most difficult to hand over? My sins. Especially the little sneaky ones that come out of my mouth as a sarcastic jab or critical comment. These are the sins that, like ninjas, quietly sneak into my thoughts and make their way down to my heart. Clearly, they've become a bad habit and hold some sort of value, otherwise I'd hand them over. Instead, they sit and smell like a wet towel you forgot about at the bottom of the hamper. Unconfessed sin is the greatest obstacle to God, filling the reservoir of our impure hearts.

Have you taken a heart inventory lately? I highly encourage you to do so. You'll be amazed. It's like cleaning out your garage or closet or that kitchen junk drawer. You uncover and discover all sorts of things you had no idea were there! For the most part, these things are useless, doing nothing but clutter and take up space, and yet we have such a hard time letting go of them, don't we? When my children were little, they were the worst when it came to letting go of things they no longer needed. Every time I filled up a garbage bag of old toys and plush animals for donation, they'd somehow manage to sneak their little hands into the bag and pull out a few old friends that they hadn't looked at or loved in years, but suddenly couldn't bear to part with. Our hearts are like this, but I promise that if you take the time to really dig up all the crap you have hidden there, you'll also see how desperate you are for Jesus to come in and give you an interior makeover.

Think about it this way: If God were your car, and your heart your garage, would you have the space to pull him in? Or is your garage so full of garbage that you'd have to keep God in the driveway because everything you don't need has taken his place?

In the words of Thomas à Kempis, "Let nothing be great in thine eyes, nothing high, nothing pleasant, nothing agreeable to thee, except it be purely God or of God." Mary was a model example of this. "My soul magnifies the Lord," she cries, "and my spirit rejoices in God my Savior" (Lk 1:46–47). To magnify is to extol or glorify, to make something appear larger than it is. God in Mary was larger than Mary. Her entire being, body, mind, and soul, glorified him. She served God alone. And I'll be honest, what I want to write next is, "Yeah, and because she was created sinless, this had to be so much easier for her to accomplish!" But was it? If given the choice, what would I choose? To be a sinner who is offered God's free gift of never-ending mercy, healing, and redemption? Or to be sinless and therefore feel the weight and sorrow of the sins of the world — the sins that take your baby from your arms and nail him to a tree? Please. I could barely hand my baby over to the pediatrician to get his booster shot. I think we know what I'd choose.

All sin matters. Especially the small ones. Don't let anyone tell you any differently. Sin disrupts God's plan for us, keeping us distracted from the one thing that matters, so we need to get serious about how we fight it. "Our world tends to minimize the destructive nature of sin," writes Joseph Langford. "We need to remember that sin brought death upon us all. Sin separated us from God. Sin brought Jesus to the horrors of the Crucifixion. Sin would be our complete undoing, but for the mercy of God in Christ." This is true not only of big sins, but of little ones as well. "It is good to remember the effects of venial sins. They wound the soul, impede the working of grace, deform the image of God, and make the rest of our actions less pleasing to God, since they no longer spring from a pure source, from undivided love."

The seemingly small sin I love and excuse the most? Talking about your life. Scrutinizing your decisions. Commenting on the way that you live. My preoccupation with your personal affairs and gift of talking about it to others flows out of my mouth as freely as the wind blows. I've gotten good at prefacing these conversations with, "This isn't gossip, it's just reality." Is it just me, or does getting tied up in knots over the lives of others feel like a colossal and dangerous waste of time? Yet it's one of our favorite things to do. And thanks to Instagram, we don't even need to be in the person's presence to ridicule them. Heck! We don't even have to know them! I love this reflection from St. Louis de Montfort: "Why then are we so much and so frequently attracted by news, curiosities, and vanity, and so little interested with God, our duties and our salvation? It is because we are indifferent to the things of eternity, and too much attached to those which pass away with time. Let us, therefore, begin to be now what we hope to be forever — occupied only with God, in God, and for God."

Like Mary, pure in heart, we must hold fast to an eternal perspective. Doing this is a gamechanger on so many levels. First, it reminds us that whatever hardship we are facing doesn't compare to what God has in store for us in heaven. Second, it keeps our eyes on Christ and off the crisis. And third, if we can do these two things successfully, we remain single-minded, and our suffering becomes a cause for joy.

How is that possible? Let's take a look at Acts 14:22. Paul encourages us to persevere in faith, saying, "Through many tribulations we must enter the kingdom of God." Other translations refer to these tribulations and hardships as necessary. That word *necessary* is the key not only to our divine purity (for the fire of our suffering burns away our filth and makes us pure and beautiful), but the key to our entire faith. If you're still trying to program your GPS with the shortest and fastest route to heaven, let me spare you the time and trouble and tell you right now that there's no such route. And yet, we all look for it. In the midst of trial, the desire to numb out and find fast relief is strong. We all do it. We all have our "I don't want to feel this pain" activity that keeps us from accepting our suffering and allowing God to purify us through the pain. For my friend, it's shopping. For my husband, it's hours of mindless scrolling on his phone. For myself, it's running on the treadmill or cleaning the kitchen. Yet when we reach for lesser things to satisfy and make us feel better, we divide our hearts and minds. We give half to the Lord, and we keep the other half for ourselves, fooling ourselves into thinking that somehow we hacked the system and found an alternate way to push through the pain. But here's the truth: God isn't going to spare any of us our suffering in time, because he wants to spare us the suffering of eternity. And eternity, I hear, is for a really long time.

Mary's there to help us bear with single-mindedness whatever God sends us. Full of grace and divine in purity, Mary said "yes" to all of God, not just the pieces she thought she could handle. And we can too. It's going to require serious cleaning up and maybe even some renovating, but just think of yourself as a really good home makeover show. There's no house the Lord can't flip, no mess he can't redeem. The suffering you endure on earth is like a power wash of grace, preparing you to stand before God with a heart so pure that it beats only for him. No matter what you've done, where you've been, or what you're going through, God wants you. Not half of you. Not some of you. All of you. Accept your suffering and lean into him. Allow him to purify you so that his light can shine in and through you, no matter your season or circumstance.

# — 11 —

# Embracing Your Cross with Blind Obedience

✝

When asked if I would fly to Iowa to film an eighteen-minute memorized talk, I panicked. Not over the talk — that was the easy part. It was the travel part that filled me with anxiety.

My husband covers all things traveling. All I need to know is the time and day we're leaving, and then I blindly follow him. He plans the trip, arranges the accommodations, reads the guidebooks, rents the car, and does all the driving. Me? I pack. And honestly, it's a good system that works well for the both of us. Nick's great at cross-referencing and finding deals, and I'm great at remembering the toothpaste and rolling our clothes. When is this system not helpful? When I'm asked to fly to Minneapolis, rent a car, and then drive two hours alone to Iowa. Then our system isn't so great.

When I finally made it to the hotel room, all I could do was whisper, "Thank you, Jesus" over and over again. Thank you for getting me from Connecticut to Iowa in one piece, and thank you for the gift of my husband. I had no idea how much I rely on him until he wasn't there to rely on. And maybe my lack of interest and involvement in our plans sounds crazy to you, but you have to understand, in these circumstances, I trust that my husband knows better than I do. I have the worst sense of direction and a fear of driving in the dark and on unfamiliar roads. But my husband? He's what Scripture would call a man of valor. He's courageous and steadfast; he's not afraid. I can pack a bag and jump in the passenger seat, having no idea where we're going because of my total trust in him. My blind obedience is born out of this confidence.

Obedience is up there with root canals in terms of popularity. Yet Jesus calls us to obey, not because he's on some power trip, but because he knows what's best for us. Adam and Eve made it clear from the start that disobedience leads to sin and death, so why is it so hard for us to obey God? Why does surrendering to him feel like the worst idea ever? Or is this just me? Because surrendering — especially to a story I don't like, with no guarantee it'll end well — goes against everything my earthly self automatically desires: things like full control, knowing the future, and a promise in writing that everything and everyone will be OK.

That right there is the problem.

I do have a promise in writing. It's called the Bible. However, the promise that I want is not the promise that God gives.

Bishop Barron calls faith "an attitude of trust in the presence of God." He says, "Faith is openness to what God will reveal, do, and invite. It should be obvious that in dealing with the infinite, all-powerful person of God, we are never in control." Our obedience to God demonstrates our faith, and our motivation should always be love, for Jesus says, "If you love me, you will keep my commandments" (Jn 14:15). However, Jesus doesn't merely suggest that we obey; he commands it. Yet obedience to God isn't only an act of worship; it's also rewarded (see Gn 22:18). Our all-powerful God promises that if we obey his commandments, we'll live with him forever in eternity. There will be no more sorrow or pain. We'll at long last be in paradise. It sounds like a good deal, yet I continue to flee from his will.

This raises two questions: How reckless is my love for God? How radical is my trust in him?

When the addiction narrative in our family had played out too long, my faith took a hit. I couldn't bring myself to be obedient, because the fear of what God was asking me to do was greater than my trust in him. It became impossible for my husband and me to have a conversation without it turning into a full blown argument. The devil was doing his best work: keeping us in confusion and chaos, shredding our faith. It was at this point in the journey that we recognized no amount of planning, intercepting, or jumping in and catching was going to cure this disease. The Lord made this very clear as I stood inside the lobby of a therapist's office: Outside of God, there was no cure. He invited me to drop my weapons, quit fighting, and walk away. And this terrified me, because I was uncertain where this command was coming from. Why would God ever command a parent to stop fighting? Was this really his voice?

Too afraid to share this with my husband, I texted a prayerful friend. She believed this was absolutely an instruction from God. He wasn't asking me or my husband to give up, but inviting us to rest. We were exhausted because we were fighting a battle that was never meant for us. The cure wasn't up to us to find. God himself was the cure, and he wanted us to put our son into his hands and trust him. And this made sense. God wasn't asking us to give up hope, but to demonstrate it. And to be honest, that felt risky. Blindly surrendering our child to a God who, in my mind, had yet to come through for us, was insanely hard and just about impossible. *Just about.*

Thank God for Mary and her example of blind obedience.

## Mary's Blind Obedience

Saint Irenaeus says, "Like Eve, by her disobedience, caused her death and that of the whole human race, so did the Virgin Mary, by her obedience, become the cause of her salvation and of that of all mankind."

All of salvation hinged on Mary's obedience.

No matter how crazy, unreasonable, or impossible it seemed, Mary said, "Yes". Nothing hindered her wild willingness to say "yes" to God: yes to hopping on a donkey while pregnant and heading for Bethlehem where she would most likely go into labor. Yes to presenting her firstborn son in the Temple, according to the Mosaic Law. Yes to getting out of bed with a newborn and fleeing to Egypt because her husband had a bad dream. Yes to encouraging Jesus to turn water into wine. Yes to taking her place at the foot of the cross where she was to witness and participate in the excruciating death of her Son. Yes to being the mother of the entire world.

Mary's surrender had to come first, and it was possible because she had radical faith, and her motivation was love. We'll never trust someone we don't know, and we'll never obey someone we have no faith in. Without faith and love we can't respond in obedience. Mary did crazy things for God because she had crazy faith and love. Nothing could thwart her response.

In Luke's Gospel, Jesus speaks of Mary's obedience to a large crowd. "As he said this, a woman in the crowd raised her voice and said to him, 'Blessed is the womb that bore you, and the breasts that you sucked!' But he said, 'Blessed rather are those who hear the word of God and keep it!'" (11:27–28).

In his General Audience address of September 18, 1996, Pope

St. John Paul II spoke of the importance of Mary's example of blind obedience:

> By her conduct, Mary reminds each of us of our serious responsibility to accept God's plan for our lives. In total obedience to the saving will of God expressed in the angel [Gabriel's] words, she became a model for those whom the Lord proclaims blessed, because "they hear the word of God and keep it" (Lk 11:28). In answering the woman in the crowd who proclaimed his Mother blessed, Jesus disclosed the true reason for Mary's blessedness: her adherence to God's will, which led her to accept the divine motherhood. In the Encyclical *Redemptoris Mater*, I pointed out that the new spiritual motherhood of which Jesus spoke is primarily concerned with her. Indeed, "Is not Mary the first of 'those who hear the Word of God and do it'? And therefore does not the blessing uttered by [Jesus] in response to the woman in the crowd refer primarily to her?" (20). In a certain sense, therefore, Mary is proclaimed the first disciple of her Son (see *RM* 20), and by her example invites all believers to respond generously to the Lord's grace. ...
>
> Mary, associated with Christ's victory over the sin of our first parents, appears as the true "mother of the living" (*Lumen Gentium* 56). Her motherhood, freely accepted in obedience to the divine plan, becomes a source of life for all humanity.

I can read and study all that I want about obedience to God, but the only thing that has ever helped me to be obedient ... is to be obedient. To take that leap. To say yes to whatever is asked of me when I don't understand, when I'm afraid, when loss, injury, pain, and even death are all possible outcomes. I'd love to write that my obedience is immediate and always precedes my need to know what comes next. Unfortunately, letting go of the pride that assures me that I know better than God has proved much more difficult than that.

As Fr. Louis Cameli writes,

> Any significant call [from God] involves cost. If it is truly significant, it redirects a person's life, demands an investment of time and energy, and realigns relationships, sometimes in painful ways. In this sense, a call that is heard and answered needs to be reaffirmed when its consequences and its cost become evident. When Mary experienced Joseph's misunderstanding, she experienced the price of her call. Her initial words of acceptance, "Let it be to me according to your word" (Lk 1:38), needed to be repeated.

Nothing stirs up fear and extinguishes faith like counting the cost. After years of running every possible outcome in my mind, I finally had to stop and ask myself the hard questions: Is God worth it? Are the pain of this cross and the uncertainty of life worth it? Sitting beside Mary, I knew the answer was a radical "yes." I did love God. I did have faith. I did want to be obedient. I was just stuck in the "what if?" I needed to stop looking at all the things that caused me to flee from obedience — things like fear, pain, sorrow, and loss — and instead, look at the people God has placed on this journey with me, especially Jesus, Mary, and all the saints.

That terrifying moment in the therapist's lobby was the beginning of my dependence on God and his ability to work all things for good. It was the day I denied myself my natural mother instinct — doing what felt good and right in the moment — and picked up my cross and followed God blindly, doing whatever he said, and trusting that while it made no sense, I was in good hands; accepting that, while this may not end well, God knows best. Mary was with me every step of the way, teaching me that true obedience to God's will over my own was going to require that I decide to be OK with the consequences ahead of time.

Here's the thing: God will call you to hard places — the exact places you marked as "I never want to go there." But more often than not, that hard place God calls us to is necessary.

What helped me to wrap my head around this was to meditate on the third chapter of Daniel. Here we encounter King Nebuchadnezzar who, in a rage over three Jews who refuse to worship the golden statue he set up, threatens to have them thrown into the white-hot furnace. But the threat of such an awful death doesn't sway them. They stand firm, obedient to God, and answer the king simply: "Our God whom we serve is able to deliver us from the burning fiery furnace; and he will deliver us out of your hand, O king. But if not, be it known to you, O king, that we will not serve your gods or worship the golden image which you have set up." And so the men are thrown into the furnace, with flames so fierce and so high that they consume the guards nearby. But as the Scriptures tell us, "[T]he angel of the Lord came down into the furnace to be with Azariah and his companions, and drove the fiery flames out of the furnace, and made the midst of the furnace like a moist whistling wind, so that the fire did not touch them at all or hurt or trouble them." All that could be heard from the furnace was the sound of one voice, singing, glorifying, and blessing the Lord.

Now, I know what you're thinking: *It ended well for them, but that doesn't mean it'll end well for me.* And trust me, I struggle with this, too. For years, my fear of "what if" had me praying an "only if" prayer: "I will do whatever you ask, Lord, only if you don't ask me to do this." Does this sound familiar? We pray prayers with conditions. We put God to the test. We try to manipulate his plan because we're utterly afraid of what might happen if we hand him everything and let him do as he wills.

I credit the Rosary with my turnaround and ability to surrender. Walking with Mary through the events of the life of Jesus, I began to understand Our Lady's role and her fierce love of the Lord. Mary was obedient to the point of her Son's death because she loved God for who he is, not what he gives. She didn't say, "Behold the handmaid of the Lord, let it be done according to your word — only if you promise my son will be OK." In total blindness, she gave God everything, and it was her obedience that would win her the crown and bring her to glory.

And yet, crown and all, it remains difficult. Every time I give my witness and encourage others to continue to trust and be obedient to the will of God, I'm approached by a heartbroken mother who can't bear the cross she's been given one minute longer. She can't see the good in any of it and is living in the fear of "what if?" This is so hard, because I can't promise anyone, myself included, that our loved ones will survive their cross. At least, not in the way that we hope for. This is devastatingly hard. But look back to those three men in the fiery furnace. Shad'rach, Me'shach, and Abed'nego didn't know whether or not they'd be OK. They didn't know whether or not they'd survive. They decided ahead of time to be obedient to God, without knowing how it all ends, because they loved him. Yes, they claimed that the God they knew and loved *could* save them, but they were committed to serving him even if he didn't save them in the way they wanted him to. They knew that he's still good.

What kind of faith do you want to have? A "what if" faith? Or an "even if" faith? My guess is that even those of us who've been hurt by a God who didn't show up in time, who didn't heal the disease, who put us in the exact spot we begged him to keep us away from … even we desire to live out of an "even if" faith. Why? Because obedience, regardless of the outcome, is freeing. Blind obedience says, "I'm not in control, and although I do not understand, I love you. I love you so much that I know you do know better, and that you'll make a way for me."

And he always does.

This is what I want. In all seasons and circumstances, I want an "even if" faith. I want to enter into whatever battle the Lord calls me to, promptly and obediently, so convinced and courageous that my "only if" prayer surrenders to an "even if" prayer.

If God calls you to hard places and doesn't show up and rescue you in the way you told him to, it doesn't mean that he hasn't rescued you. Nor does it mean he's left you to carry your cross alone. You have to make the jump, my friend. You have to put both feet in the faith pool and trust him with everything, especially with that one thing you're so terrified to let go of. We can't fool God with occasional trust. Just like Mary, we have to be all in.

But how? How can we deepen our trust to the point that obedience becomes our natural response? Joseph Langford writes:

> If trust in God is so important for our spiritual lives, how can we deepen our trust? Many of our problems with trust come because we don't understand the object of our trust. The object of trust is not the confidence that God will give, or do, or change, whatever we are asking of him. It is rather a confidence in our union with him, the firm belief that whatever is happening now is the best that could happen to advance the union.

One of the enemies of our trust is a "surface or superficial vision of our lives." Langford explains that this kind of vision occurs "when we take things at their face value and fail to see their deeper meaning." He goes on to explain that "while genuine trust leads to stability, equanimity, and serenity both in sorrow and in joy," a superficial view of things leaves us tossed about by the waves of whatever is happening to us." Think about the apostles on the boat, tossed about by the storm, and Peter taking a step out to Jesus. He manages to walk on water until he loses his trust; then he begins to drown. The storm wasn't Peter's problem. The problem with Peter was his trust amidst the storm. We need to make sure that the goal of our lives isn't to lose the cross, but rather, for God to use it. It's only by carrying it obediently that we'll deepen our relationship, making us painfully aware of our absolute dependence on him.

Saint Ignatius said, "As long as obedience is flourishing, all other virtues will be seen to flourish and to bear fruit." We see evidence of this in Our Lady. With our Blessed Mother's help, we too can say, "Behold, I am the handmaid of the Lord; let it be to me according to your word" (Lk 1:38).

## —12—

# Embracing Your Cross with Universal Mortification

✟

My spiritual director recently pointed out that, even though I was baptized as an infant, I'm actually a convert. "We're all converts," he said, "because we're always encountering."

My first conversion that I remember occurred while I was sitting on my bathroom floor, in a ball of snot and tears, wondering why life felt so awful. I was a wife and a mom, and I'd just moved across the country to live closer to my family — a ten-year dream that had finally come true. And yet, despite checking off on paper all the things that I'd dreamed of, none of it was enough. In that moment on the cold tile floor, none of it mattered. I still had this longing for a security I didn't feel. Security in my marriage, security in our financial life, security in the day-to-day grind. Everything felt like a free-fall, and I was using the world as my safety net. But grace entered in, and God showed up. He revealed to me the truth about myself, and safety, and the reason why I'd fallen so deeply into despair: I'd forgotten who I belonged to, and wasn't living the life he'd created me for. And so I took his hand, stood up, wiped my nose on my arm (because I'm classy like that), and walked out of the bathroom a new creation. Because of him.

If you've experienced the hand of God reaching down and pulling you back up to where you belong, is there anything greater? There's no deeper joy to be found than discovering that, no matter how fierce the dumpster fire you set and have taken up residence in, Jesus still comes to you when you cry out. He looks you in the eyes and says: "Yup, I know. I see. But guess what, kid? I still love you! Now, take this mercy and let's start living the holy life, what do you say? And next time, use a tissue. Because that snot on your arm is disgusting."

It has taken me fifty years, but I've finally grasped what will ultimately make my life secure. Ironically, losing my life, not saving it, is the only safe option. I have a deep-seated desire to feel safe and secure. My desire for security isn't wrong, but I've looked in all the wrong places for its fulfillment. Only God can offer security. Peace can only be found in Christ Jesus. And the goal of life isn't to remove the suffering and kick back in lounge socks. The goal is heaven, and the model Jesus left us for getting there is the cross. If there was another way, he would've shown us. We need to stop focusing on securing life here on earth and start living a life that rewards us with secure salvation. "Let your eyes look directly forward, / and your gaze be straight before you," Proverbs 4:25 reminds us. And this, my friend, will require that we die to many things we've grasped onto for far too long.

There's a Spanish proverb that describes a discontented season of my life perfectly, and (in translation) it goes like this: *Envy is thin because it bites but never eats.* During my junior year of college, I began therapy for an eating disorder. I was a mess. Having gone from a confident musical theatre major (my forever dream and plan) to "undecided," the life I was once so certain about started bleeding out. I fell hard into disappointment and comparison, unable to bear my own reflection in the mirror, because all I could see and feel was this overwhelming weight of meaninglessness and failure. I was convinced that everyone around me had it all together. They had figured life out and were paving a path to success, while I swerved to the right and to the left with envy as my guide. Despite the boyfriend who adored me and the sorority sisters who welcomed me, I hated who I was. To be more accurate, I hated that I no longer knew who I thought I was supposed to be. Feeling so out of control for the first time in my life, I fell into an eating disorder, in the hopes that I could starve away the grief of losing that girl who didn't succeed. Because you see, for the first twenty years of my life, my purpose had been tied to a dream, a loose ribbon attached to a balloon of false identity. *Who I was* had nothing to do with *whose I was*, and everything to do with what I produced. So when that plan came undone, I did, too.

When I began therapy and started unpacking all the reasons why I'd fallen into such self-hatred and destruction, I realized that putting on weight was going to have to be part of the deal if I wanted to be well. And I did want to be well. More than anything, I wanted to be happy. I hated how utterly consuming and exhausting it was to count calories, run miles, and avoid meals, but giving up that hollow, hungry, empty feeling terrified me because I knew that as soon as I started to fill myself back up, I wouldn't be able to stop. And I was right. I went from starvation to binging; there was no in between. I became a bottomless pit that couldn't be filled. The more I shoved in my mouth, the louder the deep growl within me howled. As the weight came on fast, so did the fear. Lack of control messed with my mind, and I thought the only way out of the pain was to eliminate everything I'd just consumed. Binging and purging is a miserable cycle. It's a disordered pattern that goes completely against the way God intended our bodies to work, wearing not only on the body, but the mind and soul as well. And yet, this process was necessary. I had to go through it. I had to feel and experience the suffering of an emptiness that I was never asked to fill. A space so deep and wide that no matter how much I stuffed into it, I still felt utterly empty. The only route to wholeness and happiness was by feeling and living with what I'd tried for so long to numb and kill. Once I accepted that there was no number on the scale or tag in a pair of jeans that would ever make me happy, I began to wake up to who could. It was my Red Sea, and God was inviting me to stop walking around it, and to courageously walk through it. And I did.

Our hearts have God-shaped holes in them, and try as we may, nothing but God will ever fill them. I have learned this firsthand, but I still fall into the trap of thinking that things like scented candles, clean bathrooms, renovated kitchens, and freshly cut hair will make me happy. I even turn to religious items to close the gap. Buy another rosary, collect more prayer cards, purchase another leather-bound prayer book; as if the more I accumulate for Jesus, the holier I'll be. But the Gospel tells us differently. Jesus doesn't ask us to accumulate anything other than our poverty. "Blessed are the poor in spirit," he says, not "blessed are they who have really nice prayer books."

In his *Word on Fire* podcast, Bishop Barron talks about what we need to do to save our souls:

> Jesus, in our Gospel for today, says, "Whoever wishes to come after me must deny himself, take up his cross and follow me." Do you want to save your soul? There's the formula. Find the path in your life that leads you to more and more self-emptying and self-gift, which conforms you to the love that God is. But then the Lord gets even

more specific: "For whoever wishes to save his life will lose it, but whoever loses his life for my sake will find it." Saving one's life means … filling oneself up and making oneself as safe and comfortable and sated as possible — which leads to boredom, disgust, and despair.

It's important to understand that punishing our body and emptying ourselves are two very different things. Punishing is the result of self-hatred and fear, both of which are not of God. On the other hand, fasting is motivated by love and reverence for God. When we choose to fast from food to temper our need for immediate gratification and use it as prayer, the Lord delights in our efforts. When we starve our bodies to numb ourselves from a pain we refuse to acknowledge, we're abusing the precious and beautiful gift God has given us in the body. Saint Paul writes in 1 Corinthians 6:19: "Do you not know that your body is a temple of the Holy Spirit within you, which you have from God? You are not your own." That last line is everything: "You are not your own." Why did I fall so easily into an eating disorder? Because I was having an identity crisis. And this isn't just a women's issue. According to the Brain and Behavior Research Foundation, "Despite the stereotype that eating disorders only occur in women, about one in three people struggling with an eating disorder is male, and subclinical eating disordered behaviors (including binge eating, purging, laxative abuse, and fasting for weight loss) are nearly as common among men as they are among women." Often, the way we treat our bodies and live our lives is in direct correlation to our identity, and eating disorders don't discriminate.

After my conversion on the bathroom floor, I understood, as best as I ever have, that living as a daughter of God was going to have to look different. How I lived my life was going to have to reflect the God who'd rescued me. And so, I began what I like to call my new holy habits: poring over Scripture, participating in daily

Mass, diving headfirst into Bible study, and making frequent trips to the confessional. I was determined to wipe clean everything that was offensive to God — my online presence, foul language, anything in my social media feed that I knew would not be in Jesus' social media feed. I started paying close attention to what my eyes looked at and what I fed my body. It was as if I got down on the ground, sunk my knees into the dirt, and started weeding out anything toxic that would threaten this new, virtuous me. And this was good. Really good. But it wasn't enough.

There were some weeds I just couldn't pull. And by "couldn't pull" I mean "refused to pull." Small sins and comfortable habits that I wasn't willing to let go of, mostly because I saw no real need to do so. I figured that I was holy enough. I was sorely mistaken and in dire need of another virtue Our Lady models so well: universal mortification.

## Mary's Universal Mortification

"Mortification" means putting the flesh to death. "Universal" implies all the time, and in every situation. In order to train our souls to virtuous and holy living, we need to strip our hearts of all attachment to worldly things, in every moment of our lives. We need to become masters of self-discipline and embrace self-denial, committing ourselves to God's will while crucifying all our fleshly passions.

When your love language is lounge socks, universal mortification is not only unenjoyable, it's also extremely difficult. It flies in the face of what the world preaches: that there's no need for self-denial or archaic, self-imposed penance. We have the season of Lent after all, and forty days is long enough to give up what our body demands. But is it? Is that today's going rate for eternal life? Self-denial for just forty days each year? Seems too easy.

Self-denial is tricky for a society that behaves like every day is a game of musical chairs. We aren't naturally inclined to give our chair up; rather, we run and sit down first. Here's the thing I've discovered in my pursuit of holiness: The holy life demands that we give up all the chairs. We don't put ourselves first, but last. And this is a fight. Sacrifice isn't popular, and sacrifice for the sake of pleasing God is doubly unpopular. We're surrounded by temptations and false prophets that preach an untrue gospel. "Christian" motivational speakers teach that self-reliance and self-made holiness are the way to a happy life, and that proving and striving to be the best, never settling for anything other than riding in first class, is the mark of a strong man or woman. Do you believe this? Because it isn't true.

Mother Teresa was one of the strongest, most joyful people to walk the face of this earth, and trust me, she wasn't flying first class. She wasn't even always happy, at least not in the way the world defines happiness. She lived in the filthiest, smelliest slums, caring for people most of us would walk past and hope not to make eye contact with. And here we are, recognizing what holiness demands, yet still trying to figure out how we can make our lives more comfortable. We all want to be praised for being a Mother Teresa. We just don't want her wrinkles.

We know the formula. We know that a life of excess leads to misery. We know that suffering has its benefits. But knowing we must deny ourselves, and actually denying ourselves, are two different things. How do we do this? How do we imitate this virtue of universal mortification in a world that encourages the very opposite? I find encouragement in these words of St. Louis de Montfort:

> A vigorous, constant, and generous effort to overcome ourselves, forwards us more in the ways of perfection and salvation than all those fruitless desires by which we would give ourselves to God, yet we do not what we would. The more we die to ourselves, the more do we live to God; and the more we refuse to gratify ourselves, so

much the more do we please Him. How delightful must the life of that Christian be whose desires are so regulated that his chief happiness is in denying himself, and pleasing God! How sure a means of obtaining a happy eternity!

Saint Louis continues, "To advance in virtue, we must overcome and renounce ourselves in all things and die to the insatiable desires of our heart."

I've spent a lot of time in prayer with this one sentence. What are the insatiable desires of my heart? I've pondered, examined, and begged the Lord to please uproot in me anything that wasn't of him. This poor Gardener of my soul has quite the weeding job ahead of him. If only my good fruit flourished and thrived the way the weeds do!

What are my weeds that Jesus has dug up and brought into the light? Buckle up my friend, because I am about to list them, and they weren't what I thought they'd be. That's why I want to share them — because yours probably aren't what you think they are, either. I was all set to give up good things like that afternoon bowl of blueberries and almonds, or that second pot of coffee. Or that third pot of coffee. Or time on my phone. Or that fourth pot of coffee. But a funny thing happens when you sit in the quiet and waste time with Jesus. A miraculous occurrence takes place when you ask God what he thinks you should do. *He hears you, and he answers.* What he's pointed out and asked me to give up feels as comfortable as ripping both of my arms off. It literally hurts. Denying these stupid little gratifications on a daily basis feels like a mini crucifixion. I'm not even kidding. It's a struggle. It's suffering. And it's the whole point.

Here are the things Jesus has asked me to deny myself every day, if I want to grow in the virtue of mortification:

- Needing to be right

- Explaining myself so that I'm understood
- Having the last word
- Complaining
- Avoiding the difficult decision or conversation
- Gossip
- Pride
- Envy
- Jealousy
- Sarcasm
- Useless chatter

Why is universal mortification so hard? Scripture tells us why: According to Saint Paul, "For the desires of the flesh are against the Spirit, and the desires of the Spirit are against the flesh; for these are opposed to each other, to prevent you from doing what you would" (Gal 5:17). How many of us do what we don't want? How many times do I sit in the dark and pray for the strength not to be annoyed by my husband's sniffling — only to feel annoyed when he walks into the kitchen to get his coffee ... and sniffles. (I know. How dare he!) The flesh is weak. Super weak. So fervently pursuing this virtue of universal mortification is going to require that we fight against all our passions all the time. It requires turning all occasions into opportunities for spiritual profit, and being OK with it when no one seems to notice the hard inner work we're doing. Remember, while we may be hidden from the world, we aren't hidden from God. He sees that we aren't complaining. He sees when we refrain from gossip. He sees the million and one ways we're dying, and he'll take all our suffering and make us holy.

This is what I want. More than I want to be right. More than I want to be praised. More than I want my friend's house with the amazing kitchen island. I want to be holy. I want to serve God, not the flesh, and I want to be in control of my impulses and thoughts, not the other way around. The only way that a self-gratification seeker like myself can ever advance in the virtue of universal mortification — the only way I'll ever be able to overcome all the obstacles, big and small — is by staying close to, and learning from, Mary.

Mary spent her life in mortification. Cooperating with God's plan meant letting go of her own. She embraced self-denial without complaint because she treasured the opportunity to offer her life for love of God. Think about that for a minute. Have you ever been so in love that there wasn't anything you wouldn't do for your lover? They call this "the honeymoon phase," and it lasts for a little while — until, you know, the toothpaste is squeezed from the wrong end, or the kitchen chairs never get pushed back in, or someone starts sniffling. But Mary didn't love God for a phase. She loved him forever. This is how Mary always loved: completely, fully, wholly, and without reserve. She held nothing back, knowing that earth wasn't worth gaining when compared to the reward in heaven. Mary loved God. She could deny herself everything because she knew he was all that she needed.

Too often we look at our cross from the wrong angle. We need to get under it, recognizing that the more we put to death our flesh, the stronger our spirit becomes. In *The Imitation of Christ*, Thomas à Kempis states that God promises us, "The more you withdraw from creature comforts, the sweeter and more lasting will be the comfort you find in Me. In the beginning you won't attain to these without struggle and labor; for your old habits will stand in your way, but better ones will overcome them."

St. Louis de Montfort writes in *True Devotion to Mary with Preparation for Total Consecration,* "How many Christians adore Jesus, poor in the manger, and suffering upon the cross, who will neither submit to privation, nor endure tribulation for His sake! Yet He was born, and lived, and died in poverty and sufferings, to teach us to renounce all things, and bear our cross with patience." We give up so much for lesser things, without second thought or hesitation. But when it comes to suffering for Christ, we're not so sure. When it comes to self-denial, we doubt its purpose and justify giving in to temptation.

It helps to stay grounded in the present moment. We don't have to worry about giving up all the things forever, but just this one thing right now. When Mary said yes to carrying Jesus, she wasn't worrying about all the sacrifices this would entail later on. She pondered the present moment. We can do this, too, can't we? We can say no to the little thing in front of us without thinking about that bigger sacrifice down the road. Mary's big "yes" was paved by a million smaller "yeses." God is good, and he doesn't throw us into the center of the arena naked and unarmed. He slowly trains us for battle. And he doesn't leave us to fight this war alone. He sends us the Spirit.

Saint Paul tells us: "The fruit of the Spirit is love, joy, peace, patience, kindness, goodness, faithfulness, gentleness, self-control; against such there is no law. And those who belong to Christ Jesus have crucified the flesh with its passions and desires. If we live by the Spirit, let us also walk by the Spirit" (Gal 5:22–25). Mary was possessed by the Spirit. Poor and simple, she remained hidden to the world, but seen by the Father. Obedient to God, she didn't fear losing anything in her life, because so long as she was doing her Father's will, she was happy.

Universal mortification requires that we deny ourselves first, then pick up our cross and follow Jesus. It's a call to radical conversion and holiness. And yes, it's going to hurt. But not forever. And because God truly is good, this is a choice. We don't have to accept this invitation. We can continue to live a life of excess that leads to terrible torment forever. Or we can start living a life of self-giving and emptying, which leads to the fullness of life. Mary chose the better part, and now she wears the crown.

The question is, will we wear our crown on earth, or will we wear it in heaven? How will we choose?

— 13 —

# Embracing Your Cross with Constant Mental Prayer

✝

Despite the well-known phrase "don't judge a book by its cover," I think it is safe to assume that we all do. If I were a book ten years ago, you'd probably guess that I had it all together. I was in great shape, keeping up with the current trends, and author of a popular, albeit inappropriate and snarky, blog. What most people didn't know was that behind the snark and the style, I was utterly and completely miserable. Far from the Lord, I was about to be broken open and forever changed. That's the me that I remember when I look back on that cold winter day. It was the moment when God had watched long enough and was ready to invite me into some serious interior renovating. How? By sending me a soul that radiated Christ in such an attractive way, I couldn't remain where I was. I would have to follow. I was at a Dynamic Catholic retreat, and God bless Matthew Kelly for living out his Christian vocation and revealing God in his actions and words, because Lord knows where I'd be today if it weren't for his "yes".

It was the day that I chose to take a detour from the wide path I was dying on and start walking on the narrow way, fully alive. It was a first "yes" in a string of thousands to come; the first of many opportunities that the Lord would offer me to rearrange my ways and plans and trust in his instead. It was the day I blindly chose his will over mine, and while life has yet to be the overflow of milk and honey that I pictured, it's been a gradual outpouring of more grace and mercy than I could ever humanly imagine or deserve. The Lord knows not to give me too much at a time. He spoon-feeds me grace — enough to be satisfied, but not quite filled, so that I keep desiring more.

My husband dropped me off in the parking lot, and I made my way into the hall. New to the parish, I knew no one, really, and so I sat in a row next to June, a mature woman I deemed safe. Years later, June and I remained friends, as she was better than safe — she was fiery and witty and, best of all, holy. It was a full-day re-treat, but there was one question that Kelly asked the group that's stayed with me: "How many of you pray constantly?" Only one woman shot her hand straight up in the air, and I remember Kelly laughing and saying something like, "Wow, really?" as in, "That's impossible, put your hand down." Of course, I don't know what Kelly was thinking, but I do know what I was thinking: "Nice try, overachiever." Come on, who prays all the time? I highly doubted that anyone could.

Today, I would argue differently.

Mary's final virtue, according to St. Louis de Montfort, is con-stant mental prayer. Sounds daunting, right? Something reserved for a hermit, monk, or cloistered nun. But truly, it's something we're all called to do. As Scripture commands, "Rejoice always, pray constantly, give thanks in all circumstances; for this is the will of God in Christ Jesus for you" (1 Thes 5:16–18). It's not so much a *need to do* as an *attitude of the soul*. So before you write this virtue off as only possible for those in religious life, hang with me as we dive deeper into this virtue and what it looks like, practically speaking, for you and me.

But first, I want to talk to you about my dog, Copper.

We rescued Copper after our sweet terrier, Emma, was hit by a neighbor's car and died in my arms, right at the school bus stop in front of my children. That wasn't traumatic at all. I loved Emma. Sure, she had a death wish and barked at my husband every day like he was an intruder, but she was my companion and inspiration for going on Rosary walks. That dog heard more Hail Marys whispered than most Catholics.

Copper is a very different dog. He pees on everything inside the house, can jump straight up in the air, and if we let him, he'd eat himself to death. There's no scrap Copper turns down. Unlike Emma, Copper doesn't have a fascination with running toward moving cars. His survival skills are pretty good. He does, however, have one similarity to that sweet terrier. He loves me. I mean, really loves me. If I leave for five minutes, he greets me at the door as if I were gone for ten years. Seriously, he should run the pre-Cana at all parishes. He could save a lot of marriages with his example of how to greet your loved one at the end of a long day. He sleeps with me, follows me, and is always within a ten-foot radius of me. If Copper isn't in the same room that I am, it's only because he got trapped in another room or was forgotten outside. Of course, when this happens I immediately think he's dead (because, you know, worst-case scenario and all that dog trauma). Copper is constant. He can be in a dead sleep, blanketed beneath the coziest comforter ever, but if I get up from my desk and walk out of the room, without thought or hesitation he'll wake up and follow wherever I go; no questions asked — obviously, because he is a dog. But you get the picture. No matter what Copper's doing, he's aware of my presence and he longs to be with me, every single second of the day. Constantly.

Now that you know about Copper, let's talk about constant mental prayer, because honestly — they're so similar.

## Mary's Constant Mental Prayer

Let's start with that word "constant." I know what you might be thinking. There's nothing that I do all the time. Well, what about breathing? Are you doing that? Probably. And if not, you died while reading my book, and I'm not so sure how I feel about that. But if you're breathing, you probably don't think about breathing all the time, right? You probably just breathe. The point being, maybe we can be constantly aware of God's presence — like Copper is aware of my presence — without being engaged in prayer as we tend to understand it.

When we talk about mental, think *thoughts*. That running cassette tape in your head that never shuts off. (Yes, I just gave away my age. If you are a millennial, you might want to search "cassette tape" before reading on.)

And finally, *Prayer*. Contrary to what I learned back in my 1970s felt-and-glue catechesis, prayer is more than a few "thous" and "thy wills." As I tell my religious education students, prayer is a conversation with God. St. Thérèse of Lisieux offers us a beautiful definition of prayer: "For me, prayer is a surge of the heart; it is a simple look turned toward heaven, it is a cry of recognition and love, embracing both trial and joy." Padre Pio drives home the urgency and necessity of prayer more simply: "Prayer is the oxygen of the soul."

The number one reason why people don't pray (and by reason, I mean excuse) is that they're too busy. We're not too busy to scroll through social media, watch the news, binge on Netflix, play golf, or go to pilates. But spending time with God? Still, I get it. You're busy. I'm busy. Busy is a real, actual thing. Someone has to make sure the kids' nails are clipped, that school forms are filled out, and that there's clean underwear in the drawers. If my husband didn't make runs to Costco and the dump, refinance the house, and change the battery in the car, who would? But what if we could do all these things and still be aware of God? What if we were able to transform every moment into a spiritual one? What if we were able to bring Jesus into our day and go about our business, but never lose sight of him? What if we could be like Copper: constantly aware that the one we love is never far?

Certainly, if my dog can nail this virtue, we can, too.

There is a Latin phrase I recently stumbled upon: *Coram Deo*, which means "in the presence of God." "To live coram Deo is to live one's entire life in the presence of God, under the authority of God, to the glory of God." Being aware of God in our midst is something we can learn to do constantly. Can we take the garbage to the dump and fix broken appliances while remaining aware of God's presence? After all, without God, we wouldn't have garbage to throw away, appliances to fix, or working hands and feet to make it all possible. At the very least, shouldn't we thank him?

St. Teresa of Ávila was a Spanish Carmelite nun who wrote and taught a lot about mental prayer. She mastered an interior posture of prayer that most of us barely scratch the surface of. For those of us too busy for God, convinced that prayer is only kneeling at church on Sunday, Saint Teresa sheds some serious light on how we can hear God and be with God constantly, no matter what we're doing. In her classic work *The Interior Castle*, she writes:

> This Beloved of ours is merciful and good. Besides, he so deeply longs for our love that he keeps calling us to come closer. This voice of his is so sweet that the poor soul falls apart in the face of her inability to instantly do whatever he asks of her. And so you can see, hearing him

hurts much more than not being able to hear him. ... For now, his voice reaches us through words spoken by good people, through listening to spiritual talks and reading sacred literature. God calls to us in countless little ways all the time. Through illnesses and suffering and sorrow he calls us. Through a truth glimpsed fleetingly in a state of prayer he calls to us. No matter how halfhearted such insights may be, God rejoices whenever we learn what he is trying to teach us.

I recently experienced what felt very much like Jesus' physical presence at my side, accompanied by his voice. Not an audible voice. More like a thought. This occurred on the third day of a silent retreat. After three days of no speaking, no iPhone scrolling, no television, no outside distractions, it was as if I could finally hear what Jesus was trying to teach me. I was in my ninth year of pursuing the Lord and his will for my life, but I'd yet to learn how to be alone with God. I'd yet to experience what it means to live from my soul. We must do this, you know. If we're to depend on God and listen to him, to understand that he has a concrete and holy plan for our lives, we must learn to live from the soul. When we do, we discover something amazing: God is speaking to us constantly. We're just too distracted and busy to notice.

Constant mental prayer isn't nearly as difficult as we think it is. If we could only silence our souls and learn how to rest with Jesus, our awareness of this great God who is speaking to us all the time would be prayer enough. Unfortunately, we live in a noisy world, and our hearts and minds reflect it.

There are tremendous merits and advantages for the soul that learns to be still. The more I meditate on the virtue of constant mental prayer, the more aware I become of my own sin, because I see how many opportunities there are in my day to acknowledge God's presence and to thank him and praise him for the good things he's done. But I get too tangled up in my head, forgetting that God doesn't speak to my head. He speaks to my heart. He speaks to my soul. So many sins block this grace and become obstacles that keep me from encountering Jesus. Discouragement loves to invite itself in and tries to convince me that my prayer is no good. Perfectionism dictates that my prayer is useless and ineffective unless I check all the boxes. But these are all lies, typical lies that the enemy whispers to keep us from prayer. The truth is that there is no perfect prayer, and the worst prayer is the one left unsaid.

Prayer is a means to reach God. It's not an end. It's a continuous, ongoing journey; one that is unique and individual. Your prayer journey to God might look very different from mine, and that's OK, so long as we both aim for the same destination and goal: union with God and doing his will.

The only way we can enter into constant mental prayer is by beginning our day in quiet solitude and placing ourselves before the throne of God. This is crucial, and I'll not back down from this. We must begin and end our day in prayer. We should bookend, so to speak, our daily lives with recognition of God as our center, Creator, and all in all. Yes, our entire day can be an offering. The laundry can be lifted up for a friend, and our bad back for a personal need, and we can walk our dog in an atmosphere of thanksgiving, but we still need to carve out that quality time with the Lord. We can recognize his presence in our daily activities and circumstances only when we take the time to know who he is. If we want peace and order in our day, we need to begin each day with the One who is peace and order.

Mary teaches us how to do this. She started with Jesus, stayed with Jesus, and ended with Jesus. He was her constant. We know from Scripture that Mary always took the time to consider God — who he was and how he was working — because we read that "she pondered." This was Mary's impulse in all circumstances: to think constantly about God and the good things he was doing in her, through her, and for her: to accept with both hands both joy and sorrow, knowing that each was an invitation to draw closer to the heart of God. Mary lived in this perpetual posture of pondering, which held her in an atmosphere of constant mental prayer.

As I write this, I'm looking at a beautiful Annunciation portrait that a friend once gifted me, painted by artist Henry Ossawa Tanner. This image of Mary captivates me. An art review on *Aleteia* helped me begin to understand this portrait and the impact it has on me. Joynel Fernandes, Assistant Director of the Archdiocesan Heritage Museum in Mumbai, took the feelings in my heart and put them into words:

> Henry Ossawa Tanner treats the classic Annunciation motif in a rather unconventional manner: he reckons the simplicity of the scene, rather than its theatrical recreation. In the intimacy of a chamber, Mary is portrayed as a dark-haired Jewish peasant girl, seated at the edge of her couch in a striped crumpled attire. The orderly arrangement of the room, in contrast to her bed, suggests that Mary has suddenly been awakened in the middle of the night.
>
> The blinding form of the angel is the only source of light in the room. As this infused flood of golden light falls onto Mary's face, it allures us to where fear begins to give way to contemplation and contemplation to acceptance. It arrests our attention and ignites our imagination.

There she is … the Mother of God … *thinking*. Not running her mouth, like I might've done. Not trying to figure everything out. But simply sitting in the silence and thinking. Not thinking what *if*, but thinking what *is*. *Who* is. This was Mary's spiritual habit. A habit of lifting her heart to the Lord, constantly transforming every moment into a moment of prayer. What Mary did with her thoughts, and what we tend to do with ours, are two very different things. We lose sight of God and get lost in our thoughts; Mary kept her focus on God and offered her thoughts as prayer.

What if we could do that? What if we could transform everything into prayer, praise, and gratitude? This is more than being mindful or keeping a gratitude list. It isn't about emptying ourselves for the sake of being empty. It's putting God at the center of our everything, acknowledging that every breath in our lungs is the breath of God. This is being with God.

Being isn't doing. And this is difficult for us, because when we aren't doing anything, we feel like nothing is happening. We've become terrible creatures of production; we place our worth in how much we can accomplish. This hamster wheel we jump on is one of the greatest distractions that keeps us from God and his thirst for us. And trust me: God thirsts to be with us. His heart bleeds for love of us. He just wants to sit in the quiet and gaze at us. If I hadn't experienced the power of silence for myself, I'd never have known the necessity of obtaining the virtue of constant prayer. It's like restarting your computer, organizing your bills, or deep cleaning your fridge. Learning to step into the uncomfortable quiet helps to create open space so that the Lord can enter in. And when we meet God in solitude, we can be busy with our jobs and our families or daily activities, but because we've developed this habit of inner solitude with Our Lord, we can remain present to him throughout the day. We become more receptive to his grace.

And we learn to love our cross.

I never would've written that last sentence five years ago. But since meeting Jesus in silence and making mental prayer a daily spiritual habit, something remarkable has happened. I've made peace with my cross. I'm 100 percent certain that it's Mary who's made this possible. Who better accepted the mystery of the cross? Mary literally walks with us from Jesus in the womb to Jesus on the cross, and she stands by our side and shows us that it's not only our blessings that point us to God's love, but our greatest trage-dies as well. Mary teaches us the importance of our suffering. As Langford writes, our sufferings "are essential to the revelation of God's thirst, and they help us to become more totally dependent on him. The Lord draws us to himself with two hands — with joy and pain. Seen in the light of faith, both joys and sorrows are gifts from God. And because the Cross was the place where Jesus most plainly thirsted for us, our sharing of that Cross will always be the greatest and surest place of meeting the thirst of Jesus."

And the road to this meeting place? It is paved with silence.

On that silent retreat, I asked God repeatedly to heal my son and remove his cross. I wasn't even aware that I was asking this. When I finally silenced myself, I was able to recognize that this was a prayer I was constantly praying. I was forever praying that God would take my cross away, but I never stayed around long enough to hear his reply. We weren't in a constant conversation, but a constant monologue recited by yours truly. No wonder Mary made certain that I went on this retreat. There's no doubt in my mind that it was the Blessed Mother who arranged all the details in God's plan. Even though I went kicking and screaming, like a good mother she sent me anyway. And as I sat before Jesus in the tabernacle, surprised by my own prayer that never rested, that's when I heard the voice — that inaudible but clear-as-day voice. In response to my non-stop request to heal my son, the Lord said, "And then what?"

"And if I remove this cross, Laura, then what? How will you remain close to me? What reason will you have for meeting with me? How do you suppose you can comfort others if I have no need of comforting you? How can you minister to the suffering of oth-ers, if you don't suffer yourself? You do understand that life is a succession of crosses, don't you? If I remove this one, who's to say that the next won't be heavier? Don't you see? If the cross is removed, so is the surest place of our meeting."

My constant mental prayer is no longer to rid my life of its crosses, but to embrace them. To know how best to use them. To suffer them well and, like Mary, to carry them with complete confidence in and dependence on God. And it's amazing, really. Because do you know what happened when I began to approach my cross this way? When I let go of the desire for life to be perfect and to prosper in material ways? When I rejected the lie that a joyful life is one that's free of trials? My suffering was transformed. My cross went from dark to light — not removed, but changed. No longer do I drag a cross of just wood and nails, but I embrace one covered in roses and honey. What a sweet gift the Lord has entrusted to me, and I plan on picking it up and carrying it every day of my life until at last I arrive where the cross is no more. What a sweet and glorious day that'll be! Then, and only then, will I set my cross down, when Mary opens the gates, and my Father welcomes his handmaid home.

# Works Cited

Á Kempis, Thomas. *The Imitation of Christ.* ed. Clare L. Fitzpatrick (New Jersey: Catholic Book Publishing Corporation, 1993).

Barron, Robert. *The Word On Fire Bible* (Illinois: Word On Fire Catholic Ministries, 2020).

——— "Losing One's Soul." Accessed June 16, 2021. https://www.wordonfire.org/resources/homily/losing-ones-soul/28377/.

Bartunek, John. *The Better Part: A Christ-Centered Resource for Personal Prayer* (Manchester: Sophia Institute Press, 2011).

Benedict XVI, Pope. Quoted in "Pope proposes serenity of Mary as model for peace." *Catholic News Agency*, January 1, 2013. https://www.catholicnewsagency.com/news/26298/pope-proposes-serenity-of-mary-as-model-for-peace.

Calloway, Donald H. *Consecration to St. Joseph: The Wonders of Our Spiritual Father* (Stockbridge: Marian Press, 2020).

Cameron, Peter John. *Mysteries of the Virgin Mary: Living Our Lady's Graces* (Cincinnati: Servant Books, 2010).

Cantalamessa, Raniero. *Life in Christ: A Spiritual Commentary on the Letter to the Romans* (Collegeville, MN: Liturgical Press, 2002).

De Montfort, Saint Louis. *Love of the Eternal Wisdom* (Bay Shore: Montfort Publications, 1987).

———— *True Devotion to Mary with Preparation for Total Consecration* (Gastonia: Tan Books, 2010).

Dobson, James. *When God Doesn't Make Sense* (Carol Stream: Tyndale House, 2012).

Fernandes, Joynel. "A canvas that brings together Heaven and Earth: Henry Ossawa Tanner's 'Annunciation.'" Accessed June 17, 2021. https://aleteia.org/2017/12/15/a -canvas-that-brings-together-heaven-and-earth -henry-ossawa-tanners-annunciation/.

Gaitley, Michael E. *33 Days to Morning Glory: A Do-It-Yourself Retreat In Preparation for Marian Consecration* (Stockbridge: Marian Press, 2011).

Hattrup, Kathleen N. "The cross Mother Teresa loved and carried with her." Accessed June 17, 2021. https://aleteia .org/2016/11/27/the-cross-mother-teresa-loved-and -carried-with-her/.

Keller, Timothy. "Questions of Suffering". *Job: A Path Through Suffering.* Podcast audio, Jan. 6, 2008. https://gospelinlife .com/downloads/questions-of-suffering-5565/.

Langford, Joseph A. *I Thirst: 40 Days with Mother Teresa* (Greenwood Village: Augustine Institute, 2018).

Leaf, Caroline. *Who Switched Off My Brain? Controlling Toxic Thoughts and Emotions* (Nashville: Thomas Nelson, 2009).

National Eating Disorders. "Eating Disorders in Men & Boys." Accessed May 5, 2021. https://www.nationaleatingdisorders.org/learn /general-information/research-on-males.

Philippe, Jacques. *Searching for and Maintaining Peace* (Staten

Island: Alba House, 2002).

Sproul, R. C. "What Does 'coram Deo' Mean?" Accessed June 18, 2021. https://www.ligonier.org/blog/what-does -coram-deo-mean/.

Stackpole, Robert, STD. "Part 3: Mary, Most Pure." Accessed June 19, 2021. https://www.marian.org/mary/story .php?NID=6990.

———— "Part 12: Mary, Most Obedient." Accessed June 20, 2021. https://www.marian.org/mary/story.php?NID=7083.

United States Catholic Conference of Bishops. *Catechism of the Catholic Church* (Vatican City: Libreria Editrice Vaticana, 1994).

# About the Author

LAURA MARY PHELPS is first and foremost a beloved daughter of God who needed to crash and burn before realizing it. Her first book, *Victorious Secret: Everyday Battles and How To Win Them* (OSV, 2018), teaches women how to live victoriously by finishing off their latte and putting on their spiritual armor. A blogger at Walking With Purpose and a national speaker, she writes regularly about faith, life, and the general mess the Lord saves her from at www.lauramaryphelps.com.

# YOU MIGHT ALSO LIKE

**Living Metanoia: Finding Freedom and Fulfillment in Christ**
*Fr. Dave Pivonka, TOR*
The word "repent" in Greek is metanoia — but the original Greek word means much more than just repentance. It means to change, to turn, to think differently. Metanoia is not a one-time event but a process, and as Christians we are called to live a life of metanoia. *Living Metanoia* explores what this looks like in our daily lives, encouraging believers in all walks of life to go deeper in their relationship with Jesus. In his down-to-earth, approachable style, Fr. Dave Pivonka, TOR, addresses basic topics such as who Jesus actually is (rather than who we think he is or who we want him to be); what we need to do in order to inherit eternal life; the reality of evil; and our daily call to a deeper commitment to Christ.

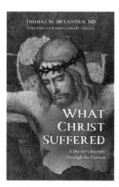

**What Christ Suffered: A Doctor's Journey Through the Passion**
*Thomas W. McGovern, MD*
This medical investigation of the Passion allows readers to enter more fully than ever into the reality of what Jesus suffered for our redemption. Drawing on the teachings of Pope Saint John Paul II in *Salvifici Doloris*, this book invites the reader to a deeper understanding of the meaning and value of human suffering — and how to practically apply it in their lives

## OSVCatholicBookstore
## or wherever books are sold.

# YOU MIGHT ALSO LIKE

**Why Are You Afraid? Have You No Faith?**
*Pope Francis*
The COVID-19 pandemic has left an indelible mark on our lives, and the same is true for the Church. Masses were suspended for months, people could not receive the sacraments, and during that time Pope Francis celebrated Mass alone every day. *Why are you afraid? Have you no faith?* collects some of the words from the pope's daily homilies when the world was in isolation during the "long Lent" in the spring of 2020, as well as Angelus messages and prayers he delivered. This book is filled with poignant photos that bring to life Pope Francis' words of support and encouragement, especially from his extraordinary blessing "Urbi et Orbi" in an empty St. Peter's Square at the Vatican on March 27, 2020. The dozens of photos in this book illustrate the themes often evoked by the Holy Father during the pandemic, including fraternal love, solidarity, the common good, and the virtue of hope. Commemorating an historically important chapter in both the papacy of Francis and the history of the modern world, this book is another avenue by which the Holy Father shares his uplifting message of wisdom, hope, and love with those who have suffered in pain, loneliness, and fear. Despite the dire challenges we have faced during this pandemic, Pope Francis reminds us that evil does not destroy confidence in God, and it does not break the solidarity of humanity.

## OSVCatholicBookstore
## or wherever books are sold.